CULTURE
The Missing Element in
Conservation and Development

Edited by R. J. Hoage and Katy Moran

National Zoological Park
Smithsonian Institution

KENDALL/HUNT PUBLISHING COMPANY
4050 Westmark Drive   Dubuque, Iowa 52002

To National Zoo director Michael Robinson and deputy director
McKinley Hudson, whose long-standing support made this
publication possible.

Published in association with the National Zoological Park, Smithsonian Institution

Chapter One: Reproduced by permission of the American Anthropological Association from
NAPA BULLETIN #15, 1995. Not for sale or further reproduction.

Printed in the United States of America

10   9   8   7   6   5   4   3   2   1

Library of Congress Cataloging-in-Publication Data

Culture : the missing element in conservation and development / edited
by R.J. Hoage and Katy Moran.
     p. cm.
     "Published in association with the National Zoological Park,
Smithsonian Institution"--T.p. verso.
     Papers presented at a symposium held at the National Zoological
Park, Washington, D.C., 1988.
     Includes bibliographical references.
     ISBN 0-7872-4761-8
     1. Nature conservation--Citizen participation--Congresses.
2. Nature conservation--Social aspects--Congresses. I. Hoage, R.
J. II. Moran, Katy. III. National Zoological Park (U.S.)
QH75.A1.C85 1998
333.7'2--dc21   98-11541
                                                                    CIP

CONTENTS

iii

FOREWORD

Throughout history, plants and animals have had an enormous impact on human culture. It was the majesty and beauty of the living world that moved Stone Age people to artistic expression. In Altamira, Spain, 20,000 years ago, humans crawled hundreds of feet underground into the belly of the earth with a sputtering oil lamp not to sketch gods and goddesses—or even anything quasi-human—but to draw animals. This is a portent of what the living world meant to human beings at that time and the effect it has had since on human culture. Stone Age artwork from the Lascaux cave in France, the Pyrenees, and North Africa is further testimony that people were inspired by animals.

Four thousand years ago an obsession with animals in Egypt was reflected in more than 40 hieroglyphic characters of animals. The animals the Egyptians chose to use in their picture-writing were highly significant. Abis, the bee, probably impressed the Egyptians because it stored food in ways that appeared logical and organized—human-like. The scarab beetle seems to have been equally interesting, most likely because it made little round balls of mammal dung and rolled them into the desert as a resource to be stored and utilized later.

For most of human history, people lived as part of the living world that surrounded them until approximately 10,000 years ago when former hunter-gatherers began to depend entirely on cultivated plants. These agriculturists began to modify these plants for human use, a practice that continues even today.

But as civilization progressed, respect for the natural world declined. Over 2,000 years ago, the last great naval battle in ancient Mediterranean times involved galleys that each took 650 trees to build. Clearly, the destruction of natural resources is not a recent development. The whole climate of the Mediterranean was changed by human activity that began millennia ago.

Today, in many parts of the world's tropics, people are burning rain forests to convert land to agriculture. The rain forest ecosystem is one of the earth's greatest centers of biological diversity. This disappearing habitat is a veritable treasure house of plant and animal species. A greater number of species lives in the tropics than in any other part of the world.

Now, as we approach the end of the 20th century, the greatest threat to life on earth is its human population. The destructive impact of human activities and technology requires us to reexamine our cultural values and search for ways to mitigate this widespread extermination of ecosystems. Most important, we need to share knowledge of effective conservation practices and environmentally sound economic development worldwide. Thus, this volume presents diverse examples of practices and programs from around the globe that have had significant implications for conservation and sustainable development. Those interested in conservation strategies—both successful and unsuccessful—can treat this collection as a compendium of valuable lessons learned.

Michael H. Robinson
Washington, D.C.

ACKNOWLEDGMENTS

The staff of the Office of Public Affairs, Mike Morgan, Marc Bretzfelder, and Susan Biggs, all contributed to the production of the symposium and this book. Thanks must go to National Zoo director Mike Robinson, deputy director McKinley Hudson, and former associate director Gretchen Ellsworth for their support of the symposia series and its proceedings volumes.

Amy Weismann, Gillian Lugbill, Jennifer McLean, Holly Harris, and Diane O'Reilly Lill edited the book's manuscript at several points in its preparation, making various writing styles consistent and readable. Production editor William Buick, Jr. completed the layout and proofing of the manuscript. Margie Gibson of the National Zoo's Office of Public Affairs provided exceptionally valuable advice, critiques, and editorial services for many of the chapters. Kathleen Spagnolo contributed several marvelous line drawings and maps.

The Friends of the National Zoo and the Smithsonian Institution provided significant funding for the National Zoological Park's symposium "Culture: The Missing Element in Conservation and Development" and the publication of this book. Many additional organizations provided support for the symposium; they include: the American Anthropological Association, Conservation International, Environmental Defense Fund, Environmental Policy Institute, Friends of the Earth, Global Tomorrow Coalition, Greenpeace USA, International Institute for Development Policy, International Institute for Environment and Development, International Union for Conservation of Nature, National Audubon Society, National Resources Defense Council, National Wildlife Federation, The Pragma Corporation, Rainforest Action Network, USAID Bureau for Science and Technology (Office of Rural and Institutional Development), Washington Association of Professional Anthropologists, World Resources Institute, and the World Wildlife Fund Wildlands and Human Needs Program.

Sarah Rogers produced the cover illustration based on an original by Richard Swartz. Kathleen Spagnolo provided the illustrations on pages 27, 29, 43, and 98, and the maps on pages 38, 80, 96, and 115. Lou Ann Dietz provided the map on page 88. The map on page 5 was adapted from *World Wildlife Fund Letter*, 1989, 7: 4, and the map on page 52 was adapted from a map provided by Benita Howell.

INTRODUCTION

R. J. Hoage, Katy Moran, and Diane O'Reilly Lill

As human activities and population growth have increased pressure on earth's ecosystems over the past few decades, conservationists have found their interests colliding with a multitude of complex issues concerning development and human needs. They have come to realize that wildlife management and captive-breeding technologies alone cannot guarantee effective conservation. To succeed today, conservationists must consider the interests of local people as well as wildlife.

The link between conservation and social and economic development was recognized as early as 1980 in *World Conservation Strategy*[1], an influential document prepared by the International Union for the Conservation of Nature (IUCN), the United Nations Environmental Programme (UNEP), and the World Wildlife Fund (WWF). Acknowledging the increasingly important role of government and development agencies in conservation, the document's authors promoted the concept of "sustainable development" as an essential conservation tool. The document's 1990 successor *Caring for the Earth*[2] expanded further on the goals of integrating conservation and development to improve the quality of human life. These ideas were emphasized once again in 1992 at the United Nations Conference on Environment and Development (UNCED) in Rio de Janeiro.

Yet while considered important, reconciling the conflicting goals inherent in improving the quality of human life and in preserving nature's diversity has proved challenging. Conservationists today still disagree on the definition and goals of sustainable development.

One area of agreement is that the needs, goals, and rights of local people must be addressed in culturally appropriate ways in order to achieve long-term conservation goals. In 1988, the National Zoological Park in Washington, D.C., hosted a symposium addressing what were then emerging issues regarding the value and importance of cultural issues to conservation and development. This volume is derived from presentations given at that conference and from follow-up discussions. It reflects early thinking on topics such as participation of local people in the design and implementation of conservation projects, the rights of indigenous peoples in natural resource management, the impact of inequitable income distribution on the environment, and cultural considerations in the design of conservation, public awareness, and education campaigns.

Since the late 1980s, the ideas presented at the symposium have matured and many of the issues addressed in the following chapters have become prominent concerns of the conservation community. For that reason, the authors of each chapter were asked to provide epilogues updating readers on recent developments. One notably active area has been the integration of conservation and economic development. Through projects that promote the concept that people living in and around protected areas must ultimately become managers of their own resources, many conservation organizations are attempting to link biodiversity conservation with local social and economic development. So far, however, most of these projects have failed to meet this simply stated but profoundly complex goal. The reason is that they have encountered many of the same problems that have plagued rural-development projects around the world for decades. The cases presented in this volume provide valuable insight into some of these problems.

One challenge has been how to include local participation in project design and implementation. Characteristically Western strategies of demarcating boundaries around fragile areas to exclude local people have proved costly and difficult to enforce in densely populated developing countries, where such an approach is completely foreign to the ways and customs of the local people. Michael Wright addresses this issue with a discussion of a conservation initiative in Zambia that attempts to balance national-level management with local participation. The success of this initiative lies not in its technical characteristics, but in its reliance on African culture and value systems.

Jere Gilles also stresses the importance of local participation in his discussion of failed range management initiatives in developing countries. He argues that degraded rangelands have been caused by blind attempts to implement modern Western techniques on pastoral systems and their managers without regard for traditional management practices. Similarly, Rasanayagam Rudran describes the importance of cultural sensitivity to the design of conservation strategies in Sri Lanka, where he has found that ancient cultural perceptions are in place and that conservation programs are most successful when these perceptions are considered and incorporated.

Local participation is relevant to conservation not only in developing countries. Benita Howell describes citizen involvement in the planning and management of national recreation areas in the Appalachian region of the United States. She discusses the social, economic, and political climates affecting government conservation decisions and shows, once again, that local participation is essential to achieving long-term conservation goals.

Many conservationists believe that local participation is only a first step. Ultimately, local people should become managers of their own natural resources, a goal of many projects described in this volume. Achieving effective local management is not easy, however. One reason is that governments and conservation and development organizations have their own agendas and are reluctant to compromise their interests, especially when the management techniques of local resource users are different and difficult to comprehend. An unfortunate result has been many cases where government intervention or privatization in the name of conservation has degraded local environments by undermining communal regulation of access to resources. Bonnie McCay, for example, has studied commercial fishermen of Canada and the eastern seaboard of the United States. She learned that conservationists must appreciate the social and cultural conditions under which people cooperate to protect the resources they value, even if the goals may initially appear incompatible with conservation.

Beyond the need to be culturally sensitive, it has recently become clear that many conservation efforts will succeed only if they can "pay their own way." In other words, wildlife and wild habitats stand a much better chance of survival if people derive economic benefits from their existence. Economics has shaped many recent conservation efforts, including techniques applied in Thailand's Khao Yai National Park, which are described by Jeffrey McNeely. After attempts to conserve the park through force of law failed miserably, the needs and wants of local people were taken into consideration. The long-term outlook for the park greatly improved.

Through the development of education and public-awareness campaigns that respect cultural values, local people can be empowered to manage their natural resources in an ecologically sensitive manner. Lou Ann Dietz discusses the success of the golden lion tamarin project in Brazil, a project that emphasizes the need for local leaders to communicate with the public in culturally appropriate ways. The project has not only drawn positive attention to the community and its conservation projects, but has linked the needs of the community to long-term conservation goals.

Despite increasing awareness of the importance of accepting alternative cultural values, lack of cultural sensitivity continues to undermine many conservation attempts. There is a Western tendency to romanticize indigenous peoples and to underestimate the value of their models of natural-resource management. For example, Harvey Feit describes fundamental cultural differences between the James Bay Cree and the Canadian government in their effort to co-manage the resources in northern Quebec. Darrell Posey also addresses the issue of indigenous rights with a discussion of the Kayapó in Brazil and the threats of Western exploitation of their traditional knowledge of conserving tropical ecosystems. Stewart Hudson details the early formation of an alliance between the Coordinating Body for the Indigenous Peoples' Organizations of the Amazon Basin (COICA) and the environmental community in North America. In all of these examples, insensitivities to fundamental cultural differences have resulted in turmoil and, in most cases, environmental degradation.

Perhaps the greatest problem associated with conservation and development is the unequal distribution of wealth on both global and local scales. Michael

Painter specifically addresses this concern with a discussion of the tremendous inequity in access to natural resources that underlies environmental destruction in the Amazon Basin. Katy Moran takes a broader look at this issue with her discussion of debt-for-nature swaps, arrangements through which indebted developing countries exchange portions of their foreign debt for measures that protect the environment.

As we face a world population of six billion at the start of the coming century, resource distribution and the development of environmentally sustainable ways of living will only become more significant issues. The case studies presented in this book support the idea that successful conservation activities depend on the cooperation and mutual understanding of all concerned peoples. Conservationists must learn about and appreciate the cultures and traditions of local people as well as their goals and aspirations for the future. Culture is dynamic, and the contributors to this volume suggest that its energy must be harnessed to achieve long-term solutions to conservation problems. Only then can the world community begin to deal with what may be the greatest challenge for the coming century: effectively reconciling the needs of people—including their cultural values and traditions—and the survival of the world's diminishing wildlife and wildlands.

---

[1] *World conservation strategy: Living resource conservation for sustainable development.* International Union for Conservation of Nature and Natural Resources (IUCN), United Nations Environment Programme (UNEP), World Wildlife Fund (WWF), United Nations Food and Agriculture Organization (UN FAO). Morges, Switzerland: IUCN, 54 pp.

[2] *Summary: Caring for the Earth: A strategy for sustainable living.* IUCN, UNEP, WWF. Gland, Switzerland: IUCN, 24 pp.

CHAPTER ONE

ALLEVIATING POVERTY AND CONSERVING WILDLIFE IN AFRICA: AN "IMPERFECT" MODEL FROM ZAMBIA

R. Michael Wright

The Perfect Model That Never Was

> Whenever the British have undertaken the development of a new country, amongst the earliest regulations will nearly always be found a measure which is designed to afford a degree of protection to the local fauna. It is a pleasing British characteristic. Accordingly, since the last years of the 19th century the well-being of much of East Africa's splendid wildlife was carefully fostered by regulations, which not only puzzled the indigenous population, but was an irritant. (Speech of Captain Charles R. S. Pitman before the Mammal Society of the British Isles, March 27, 1960, quoted in Marks 1984.)

Nature's eternity is symbolized in the pristine African plains teeming with spectacular herds of wildlife: wildebeest from horizon to horizon, majestic lions roaming among stately giraffes, scampering warthogs, their tails erect, and hyenas skulking through the underbrush. In this popular image, the African landscape is generally devoid of the African people.

The problem is rooted in the nature of the colonial relationship itself, which allowed Europeans to impose their image of Africa upon its reality. Beyond economics, much of the emotional investment Europe made in Africa manifested itself in a wish to protect the natural environment as a special kind of "Eden"—a paradise for the European psyche rather than a complex and changing environment in which people actually live.

This early history would be of only passing interest were it not for the astonishing continuity in policy from the colonial state to the independent governments of modern Africa. The mythology of the African environment and the symbol of Africa as a yet unspoiled Eden also continues to stimulate many outsiders who wish to intervene in the way its environment is managed (Anderson and Grove 1987). The myth is maintained today through a deluge of beautiful coffee-table

1

books and widely popular television specials on African wildlife and habitats. Continued enthusiasm for outside intervention was seen most recently and dramatically in calls from the capitals of Europe and the United States for a ban on all trade in elephant ivory—even for those countries such as Zimbabwe and Botswana, which have successfully managed their elephant populations.

Some have argued that the "Eden" European mythology sought to preserve never existed at all. Colonists arriving in East Africa in the 1890s found what appeared to be a vast, empty paradise, unaware that the reason may have been smallpox, which devastated the human population, and rinderpest, which had annihilated the cattle (Deihl 1988). Disease-related disasters occurred elsewhere on the continent: in the Belgian Congo, for example, a population of 40 million in 1880 declined to 9.25 million by 1933 (Bell 1987). Against this backdrop, the "hunting-mad, animal-loving British" and, more recently, African national governments have set aside considerable areas for the protection of wildlife and natural habitats. In Tanzania, Botswana, Zambia, Zimbabwe, Senegal, and even Rwanda—one of Africa's most densely populated countries—these protected areas cover more than 10 percent of the gross land area. Whereas the first U.S. national parks were established to preserve monumental landscapes, the African protected areas focused from the start on wildlife, initially preserving the royal hunting prerogative from colonizer excesses and, after World War II, turning toward nature preservation. Although motives for their creation changed over time, these protected areas were nearly always carved out of communal tribal lands whose populations were treated, more often than not, as irrelevant.

Just as park lands were alienated from the communities and maintained solely for the use of the government, so, too, did the colonial regimes reserve wildlife for the use of the ruling white authority. While after independence the racial makeup of the beneficiaries changed, the animals remained the property of the state, and revenues generated from safaris and other uses of parklands went to the national treasury. In response, rural subsistence farmers who coexisted with wildlife developed a pattern of uncontrolled illegal use. Wildlife became a classic case of an open-access resource as local people perceived little likelihood of any future benefit from deferred use. The government, on the other hand, claimed exclusive ownership but lacked the political, financial, and human capacity to enforce regulations and protect the resource.

The Price of Perfection

> [The Ik] too were driven by the need to survive against seemingly invincible odds, and they succeeded, at the cost of their humanity.... The Ik have relinquished all luxury in the name of individual survival, and the result is that they live on as a people without life, without passion, beyond humanity (Turnbull 1972).

The Ik, banished from their traditional hunting areas and forced to scratch out something resembling a life on barren hillsides, are just one of the better-documented examples of the social and cultural disintegration of a people expelled to make way for a protected area. Similar examples are found throughout Africa, including the San Bushmen (Volkman 1986) and the Masai (Parkipuny and Berger 1993), as well as outside the African continent (Gardner and Nelson 1981; Clay 1985; Lawson 1985; Poole 1989). As William Partridge (in press) demonstrates in his analysis of involuntary resettlement, both development proponents and conservationists have largely ignored the social consequences of their actions. Often made as though there were no people in Africa, conservation decisions have deprived rural peasants of land, traditional food sources, and the ability to trade in wildlife products and have severed key cultural links that hunting played in many societies. Rural people have also been forced to compete with wildlife for grazing and water and to endure crop destruction and loss of human life. The simple fact is that, except for the financial costs of administration, the burden of Africa's extensive protected-area system has fallen on the poor rural population while the inspirational, educational, recreational, and scientific benefits have accrued primarily to foreigners and the prestige and revenues to national governments (Bell 1987).

The human cost of the loss of land to protected areas has escalated as sub-Saharan Africa's population has grown—an increase of 80 million people between 1970 and 1985. A shrinking land base for subsistence agriculture, overgrazing, and a shortage of fuel wood have all led to deforestation and soil erosion in a region in which the carrying capacity has already been exceeded in many of the more arid countries. Deterioration on their peripheries has damaged the integrity of the protected areas themselves, as most suffer from design flaws such as boundaries that cut across ecosystems, migration routes, and traditional wildlife grazing areas.

As rural Africans' own resource bases deteriorate, the parks become ever more attractive and exclusion through punitive measures becomes ever more financially and politically costly. Here lies the seeds of destruction of Africa's Eden and the link that makes the villager and poacher allies. The future of protected areas and conservation of wildlife outside park borders—and perhaps within them as well—depend on solving two problems: First, can enough resources be provided to allow farmers outside parks to make a reasonable standard of living? Second, can institutions to protect wildlife be found or created that tap the enlightened self-interest of African people themselves? Conservation strategies will be enforced by them only if they are grounded in the traditional social structure of rural Africans rather than through a central policing system that few governments can afford. This issue defines the role of and challenge to the anthropological profession in the conservation movement.

An "Imperfect" Alternative

> Better to let them do it imperfectly than to do it perfectly your-
> self, for it is their country, their way, and your time is short
> (Lawrence of Arabia).

Culturally-based ecosystem management systems (Matowanyika 1989) must be developed that link conservation to a process of rural development and to the survival of agrarian societies in Africa. Particularly needed are alternatives that look at the wildlife resources flowing out of and surrounding parks as a basis for community management systems. Only a culturally-based conservation system that meets both ecological and social criteria can succeed in Africa. While conventional development has often ignored the ecological criteria, until recently conservationists have ignored the social and cultural parameters.

In conventional development thinking, wildlife is considered a less reli-able resource than domesticated animals. Wild species, however, have definite ecological advantages over traditional livestock. In semi-arid savannas they are more selective in their grazing preferences, are more tolerant of droughts, and are less likely to degrade the productive potential of ecosystems than cattle. These same multiple values can be realized at lower stocking levels, thus posing less risk to ecosystem stability. As we are now learning, wildlife can have a comparative economic advantage that has been distorted by a subsidized pricing and marketing system prejudiced toward cattle (Child, Graham, and Nduku 1985).

Systems using wildlife have become well established on private ranches in Zimbabwe (Cumming 1987) and, to a lesser extent, Kenya (Hopcraft 1986). Commercial ranchers have found that harvesting wildlife can be more profitable than cattle under semi-arid conditions on marginal land, an advantage made even greater when foreign-exchange factors are considered. As a result, a majority of commercial cattle ranchers in Zimbabwe now devote at least some of their lands to wildlife, which often provides 25 to 50 percent of net income. Contrary to the enthusiastic claims of some wildlife ranching proponents, the Zimbabwe experi-ence indicates that wildlife is not generally a cheaper source of protein than do-mestic stock (although in some instances it can produce comparable meat with less risk of ecosystem degradation). The real economic attraction is that wild popu-lations can sustain an array of simultaneous income-generating uses—culling or cropping for meat, preparation or marketing of wildlife products, safari hunting, and nonconsumptive uses such as game viewing and photographic safaris. Such diversification without intensification of resource use is the essence of sustainable development (Muir 1988; Development Alternatives 1989).

Can these experiences with private lands be translated to communal pro-prietorship in areas adjacent to and surrounding national parks and protected ar-eas? For millennia, wildlife hunting has been a major component of the diets of

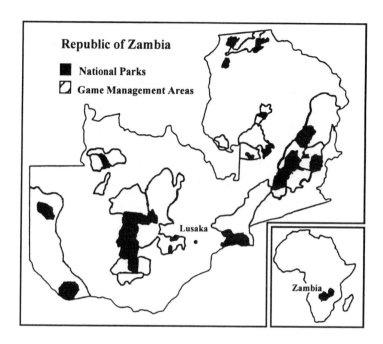

Figure 1.1. Zambia and its wildlife preserves. Derived from *World Wildlife Fund Letter*, 1989, 7: 4. (Adapted from image designed by University of Maryland Cartographic Services.)

rural communities in Africa and elsewhere in the developing world (International Union for the Conservation of Nature 1981; Caldecott 1986; Redford and Robinson 1987; Clay 1988). The use of wildlife for protein in western and central Africa has been particularly well documented (Asibey 1974; Hart and Petrides 1987; Ntiamoa-Baidu 1987). Tribal social structure and culture in southern Africa also include patterns of allocating and managing wild species, which were disrupted during the colonial period (Murphree and Murombedzi 1987; Selpapitso 1988; Cumming and Taylor 1989; Hitchcock 1989; Owen-Smith and Jacobsohn 1989). In many parts of rural Africa these traditional authority structures, though seriously weakened in the early independence period, are still in place and could be revived by regimes of local wildlife proprietorship. From the conservation viewpoint, giving local communities a stake in wildlife could do much to discourage poaching and reverse the currently adversarial relationship between government ministries responsible for wildlife protection and their poor human neighbors.

Practicing the "Imperfect"

Experience with community participation in conservation confirms what we already know, namely that wildlife resources are wealth. But the significance of the approach lies in the fact that it ensures that this wealth is used to benefit the people to whom the resources belong instead of satisfying the individual and self-ish needs of an indiscriminate poacher.

That is how, in July 1989, Dr. Kenneth D. Kaunda, then president of the Republic of Zambia, described the Administrative Management Design for Game Management Areas (ADMADE), one of the growing number of African experiments seeking a balanced approach to wildlife protection. Developed by the Zambia National Parks and Wildlife Service over the past eight years, ADMADE is a national program built upon the experience of the Lupande Development Pilot Project (LDP).

The Setting

Zambia contains some of Africa's largest remaining concentrations of savanna wildlife, and isolated rural populations depend heavily on these resources. The country, therefore, has the potential to design a multiple-use conservation approach that is an inseparable part of its traditional culture. Zambia has a system of 19 national parks covering 8 percent of the nation (Figure 1), which the government seeks to manage according to strict protection standards. Buffering these parks are 32 game management areas (GMAs) covering an additional 22 percent of the country. While GMAs were established for multiple use and local human benefits, without a government extension program, they have not yet contributed significantly to local economies.

An exception is in the Luangwa Valley in eastern Zambia, where the LDP is located. The valley contains about 25,000 elephants and a remnant population of black rhinos, as well as large numbers of buffaloes, hippos, crocodiles, and a full range of predators and small game. The valley has four national parks surrounded by sparsely settled GMAs, which together cover some 80 percent of the catchment area containing significant wildlife populations and supporting an important safari hunting industry. Most of the 40,000 people of Luangwa Valley from five distinct tribes are poor subsistence farmers living in scattered villages along alluvial drainages. Social services such as schools and health centers are inadequate, and malnutrition and protein deficiencies are common. Little investment has been made in agriculture, and development projects have passed them by. The area is infested with tsetse fly, and soil conditions make only 3 to 7 percent of the land arable. Nonetheless, these lands must somehow accommodate a growing population and its need for food (Marks 1984). The World Wildlife Fund (WWF), through its Wildlands and Human Needs Program (Wright 1988), has supported the expansion of the LDP, which serves as a pilot program and training center, into nine other GMAs.

Evolution of ADMADE

The most important precursor to ADMADE was the Lupande Development Workshop held at Nyamaluma in September 1983. Addressing workshop participants, Chief Malama complained bitterly about the lack of benefits from wildlife on his land:

> We are honest people who are keepers of the wildlife. We do not like poaching and we have been keeping the animals here a long time for the Government, but we receive no benefit for this service. If I beg help for building a clinic or grading our road, the government refuses. Yet, this is the area where both the government and private individuals benefit from wildlife. Tourists come here to enjoy the lodges and to view wildlife. Safari companies come to kill animals and make money. We are forgotten (Malama 1984).

These complaints were well-founded, as less than 1 percent of safari hunting revenue was returned to local economies (1984). Although the complaints were neither new nor confined to Zambia, they found a responsive ear in Gilson Kaweche and Akim Mwenya, then chief research officer and acting deputy director, respectively, of the National Parks and Wildlife Service (NPWS), and Dale Lewis, who was conducting elephant research with support from the New York Zoological Society. Lewis had begun to listen to local communities after hostile encounters with Chief Malama, who feared that the elephant research was an excuse to expand the adjacent park (Lewis 1989). Mwenya and Kaweche had been smarting under international criticism of NPWS management of Zambia's parks (much of it from former colonial wardens) and from the partial dismemberment of the department to establish privately funded antipoaching forces such as the Save the Rhino Trust. (These attempts at international policing proved to be equally unsuccessful in stemming the slaughter of elephants, which suffered annual losses of 6 to 8 percent during the 1970s and early 1980s. In the same period, rhinos were virtually eliminated.)

Aware of similar concepts being explored in Zimbabwe through the CAMPFIRE program, the LDP was undertaken as an experiment in grassroots, community-based wildlife use and led to the creation of ADMADE.

The Lupande Development Workshop also resulted in a consultancy that developed the Luangwa Integrated Resource Development Project (LIRDP 1987). A more classic, large-scale integrated project involving sustainable use of agriculture, forestry, fisheries, water, and wildlife, the LIRDP operated in the South Luangwa National Park and the Lupande Game Management Area with major funding from NORAD, the Norwegian government's foreign-assistance program. Despite their differences in scale, approach, and budget, the two programs suffer some sibling rivalry as a result of their physical proximity, common roots, and differing relationships with central government departments.

Two government decisions in 1983 inadvertently provided the institutional basis for a new approach to wildlife management in Zambia. Faced with falling copper prices, the country's major export and foreign-exchange commodity, and a resulting difficulty meeting recurring costs, government agencies were encouraged to seek alternative funding mechanisms. In response, the Wildlife Conservation Revolving Fund was established authorizing the NPWS to generate and retain revenue and, most important of all, giving the department autonomy over the use of funds it generated. The revolving fund provided the critical legal mechanism by which NPWS shares money generated in a GMA with its residents.

Of equal importance, the minister responsible for wildlife designated all classified employees as wildlife officers. The apparently esoteric decision that nongovernment employees could be taken on as wildlife officers made possible the development of the Village Scout Program, which employs local villagers and has substantially increased law enforcement, wildlife censusing, and data collection in GMAs. Ordinarily, local villagers would not qualify for government civil service nor would it be possible for traditional chiefs to be involved in their selection. Village scouts have become a significant—and often the only—source of employment in rural areas, and, unlike NPWS employees, they can be terminated for nonperformance and are therefore highly motivated.

Structure of ADMADE

In sharp contrast to the colonial or traditional conservation approach, ADMADE is based on the belief that effective conservation and wildlife management depend upon individuals and communities who share their land with wildlife becoming full participants in decisions concerning the management and development of the resource and receiving a major share of the revenue derived from its exploitation. To be ecologically sustainable, some of these revenues must be set aside to support formal wildlife management programs. Without such investments in monitoring and maintaining the resource base, it will inevitably deteriorate. The ADMADE structure seeks to balance NPWS's national-level management responsibility for wildlife with local participation. The main features of the ADMADE program are:

- Each GMA and/or hunting block constitutes a wildlife management unit. A civil servant member of NPWS is the unit manager, and staff include NPWS wildlife officers and local village scouts.
- For every wildlife management unit there is a wildlife management authority. The authority's chairman is the district governor. Its membership includes both political and traditional leaders, including the ward chairmen, chiefs, members of Parliament, and local technical officers. The authority serves as the policy body of the unit. Links to political and traditional leadership provide opportunities to mobilize resources beyond those of NPWS to implement village community projects.
- To ensure that decision making is based on grassroots needs and priorities, every chiefdom within a unit has a wildlife management sub-authority. Its membership includes party branch chairmen, headmen, teachers, the unit leader as secretary, clinical officers, and the chief as chairman. The subauthority determines projects to be funded out of the 35 percent of the revenue available for the community.

Revenue generated through safari hunting and any other forms of wildlife utilization is held by the revolving fund and apportioned as follows: 40 percent to the local resource management programs, including employment of local villagers as scouts; 35 percent to village community development; 15 percent to NPWS operation costs; and 10 percent to ADMADE administration.

Implementation

During 1988 the WWF program focused on supporting the LDP as the pilot for ADMADE as well as its replication in five other GMAs. Within the LDP, the area patrolled by local village scouts trained and employed under this program increased by 30 percent over the previous year. A 90 percent drop in commercial poaching and a decrease in snares used for subsistence hunting indicated growing local acceptance. Decreased poaching can be attributed in part to village scout patrols and to local leaders (particularly village headmen) as the program decision body. While the company that had bid successfully for the safari concession had not yet attained the ADMADE-mandated requirement of 80 percent local employment, it had established a constructive dialogue with the community and supplied low-cost meat. Also in 1988 a small-scale, locally based culling and tanning program supported by Africare employed 20 permanent staff, putting K 6,000 (U.S.$1,500) per month in salaries into the community (in addition to 40 percent of the annual profits) (Kapungwe and Lewis 1989). Ecological monitoring continued to provide a baseline against which to judge the ecological sustainability of the pilot project.

The ADMADE replication process also began in nine GMAs (five under the WWF Wildland and Human Needs Program) in 1988. Based on the LDP model, it was estimated that about $50,000 per year would be needed to make a GMA self-sustaining (including capital replacement costs). At that time most GMAs in the ADMADE program averaged $30,000 in income exclusively from safari concession fees. The program, therefore, focused on expanding income sources, including multispecies-wildlife utilization and small-scale tourist enterprises, over the next few years. In addition, as a condition of increased U.S. Agency for International Development (USAID) funding, the Zambian government agreed that a portion of other safari revenues that went to the central treasury, such as trophy and license fees, would henceforth be shared with the communities where the revenue was earned. NPWS hired two local staff biologists in 1988 to provide logistical and technical support to unit leaders in the field, and made plans to hire a social scientist in 1990. During this period, 19 unit leaders were trained at Nyamaluma, as were 200 village scout recruits selected by their chiefs. On July 14, 1989, Zambian president Kenneth Kaunda handed over to nine chiefs checks from the revolving fund of K 2.3 million (U.S.$230,000) representing their share of the revenue derived from game in their areas. The ceremony represented the culmination of the first phase of Zambia's new approach to wildlife conservation.

Discussion

Although the Zambia Wildlands and Human Needs Project is still evolving, several principles have emerged from the experience (Lewis et al. 1990).

First, local leadership is irreplaceable. Few projects succeed without responsive and motivated leaders; in the case of ADMADE, project success relied particularly on the traditional leadership of chiefs and/or headmen as well as on the customs that bind and regulate village communities. While conservation undertaken by central governments and imposed by force has proved costly and ineffective in far-flung rural areas, integrating technical and capital inputs from these governments with traditional rulers working with local communities has in most chiefdoms proved an effective partnership.

In Latin America, local nongovernmental organizations (NGOs) play a key role in wildlands and human needs projects. But in some areas, particularly in Africa, internationally supported NGOs and expatriate experts can usurp government authority and erode the confidence and morale of both local professionals and village leaders (Ward 1989). Thus, in ADMADE, it is the traditional structure that has played the role that NGOs provide in Latin America. Beyond community leadership, the central government leadership relies on Zambian professionals rather than swelling the number of foreign experts. Africa already has the largest number of foreign experts per capita in the world—in one estimate 80,000—even exceeding the number during the colonial era (Hancock 1989). Nevertheless, the base of Zambian leadership remains exceedingly narrow and represents an institutional point of vulnerability.

No goal of ADMADE is more important than community participation. Only through this mechanism can it be ensured that projects are culturally acceptable, sensitive to local needs and aspirations, and responsive to customary laws. The classic approach to conservation, which attempts to exclude human population from strictly protected areas through police action, requires expenditures of between U.S.$200 and $250 per kilometer to be effective (Bell and Clarke 1984). The LDP achieved a 90 percent reduction in elephant poaching at a fraction of that cost ($22/km) (Lewis et al. 1990). If one dare generalize from such a limited sample, wildlife protection costs appear to be inversely related to local participation and benefit. One reason is that local village scouts have superior knowledge of areas to be patrolled and lower absenteeism than civil servants. Participation and local employment generate a multiplier effect by taking advantage of Africa's still-prevalent "economy of affection," in which the first goal of many successful Africans is to take care of and satisfy the family and the village. The fact that most poachers in the pilot project area come from outside the valley encourages proprietorship of local resources; however, it also raises questions about the replicability of this experience in those areas where poachers are primarily local.

Despite ADMADE's laudable record of local participation, women have not played an equal role. The project has disproportionately benefited men in terms of jobs and bolstered male domination of community decision making. Although women's traditional roles have not included management and utilization of large mammals, women are responsible for providing food, firewood, and medicines and are the primary users of natural resources. In addition, women who are in charge of subsistence agriculture suffer more from wildlife depredations in village gardens. This inequity still needs to be addressed within ADMADE (Hunter et al. 1990).

ADMADE's success ultimately will depend not on meeting the WWF's objectives, or even those of NPWS, but on responding to the needs of the communities themselves. Those needs, be they jobs, income, or protein source, must reach a critical threshold at least approximating the cost of conservation. If the number of beneficiaries is too small, resentment will emerge. Yet as the pilot project has demonstrated, once a threshold level of satisfaction is reached, peer pressure should in theory take over (Lewis et al. 1990).

Modest voluntary contributions from local people, including labor for the Africare culling program and in-kind or locally raised cash, demonstrate that projects addressing perceived local needs increase the sense of ownership and long-term commitment. Give-away projects or subsidized labor discourage self-reliance and distort the development process. In contrast, village employment in the ADMADE program is directly linked to and paid for by use of the wildlife resource.

Nevertheless, a project that has local leadership and community participation, and that responds to local needs may still fail due to an inappropriate legal, institutional, or policy structure. To prevent this, ADMADE is composed of a mixed system including elements of both the common property resource management and government co-management. Key institutional decisions to date have included: setting up a revolving fund and making it possible to hire nongovernment employees; getting a government commitment to return a substantial portion, if not all, of the revenue from the safari industry to the local community; and sharing control over the wildlife resource. The longer-term question for ADMADE is whether its mixed local-national/private-public approach is able to create true proprietorship over the resource at the community level and at the same time escape problems of bureaucratic inefficiency and corruption.

ADMADE incorporates several characteristics known to contribute to successful grassroots development. First, the risk to participants is minimal, requiring little up-front cash and providing a near-term payoff. Whenever possible, the required resources are already available to the poor, recurring costs are low, and income generation is focused on a reliable, stable market able to support increased production. The safari market, for example, seems capable of substantial expansion unless it is undercut by the growth of animal welfare and antihunting sentiment outside Zambia or by internal corruption of the licensing system and resource depletion from resident hunting. Capital costs are kept low. This importance of this characteristic was demonstrated by the Africare-supported self-help culling project. When an anthrax outbreak interrupted the program, there was no danger of external pressure to continue operations in order to pay off loans. Despite the loss of revenue in 1987, total revenue in the pilot project exceeded management costs almost four times. About half of the money was used locally, and the other half retained by the central treasury.

Like many development projects, a risk arises from WWF and USAID support of ADMADE. External donor support can damage cultural integrity, local self-confidence, and motivation. Projects relying on external funds may only progress when such funds are available and may require inflated budgets to meet the support levels required by foreign donors. Ultimately, larger budgets may not be sustainable without depleting the wildlife resource. In the meantime local effort can appear insignificant. In 1987, for example, local wildlife-related employment generated K 70,212 (U.S. $17,553), and a further K 63,600 (U.S. $15,900) was earned toward local community-development projects. Although substantial in an otherwise cashless economy (and, more important, locally generated and available for the indefinite future), such an amount is easily denigrated amid discussions of millions from bilateral or multilateral donors.

Based on a continual dialogue with participants, successful community projects must be flexible, creative, and able to adjust and grow based on experience and changing needs. In ADMADE, village meetings play a critical role in soliciting views and criticisms from local residents on wildlife management, both to build a sense of proprietorship and to overcome past antagonism with the NPWS. Resources must be sufficient to generate the income to meet community-identified needs. Because wildlife is subject to drought, epidemics, and habitat disruption—all of which affect reproductive success—ADMADE faces an inherent risk. A severe drop in wildlife resources due to such natural fluctuations could harm the economic sustainability of the program. For conservation to succeed, there must be a clear link between the revenues and resources. One concern with the larger-scale, integrated LIRDP from the start was that commingling of resources from different development activities—such as forestry, farming, and wildlife—may blur the wildlife stewardship and income-generating relationship sought in ADMADE.

Faced with massive needs, both human and natural, it is tempting to attack Africa's problems at once and on all fronts. However, incremental improvements carry less risk than radical changes or multiple innovations. Incremental improvements also increase prospects for success, which in turn instills self-confidence and enthusiasm. Small steps more easily balance the need for change with respect for tradition. Demonstration is critical to allow programs to prove themselves, especially given past antagonism with the government wildlife department. This approach requires patience and a focus on projects where prospects for success are greatest. ADMADE, for instance, did not start with a depleted Game Management Area, but rather asked such questions as these before beginning: Where is the best wildlife resource? The best unit leader? The most committed local chief or provincial governor?

Underlying experiences like ADMADE is the simple truth that conservationists need to find ways of doing things that will make local communities the owners of their own development and the owners of their own conservation.

The Search for "Imperfection"

Does the failure of wildlife conservation in much of Africa simply mirror a wider range of externally promoted initiatives contributing to the 1980s being Africa's "lost decade?" An increasing number of Africans argue that, whether borrowed or thrust upon them from the East or the West, they have been following the wrong model of development, and the continent must now begin to search for its own solutions. Similarly, if successful African conservation strategies are to be built, they cannot be based on a Northern mythology of an African Eden, but must be based on a clear-eyed critique of past failures and a search for African leadership and local experience. Ironically, externally promoted "ideal" approaches to conservation have long been supported at the expense of practical local solutions. ADMADE's experience in the late 1980s and early 1990s reveals the complexity and susceptibility of local solutions to political manipulation, moribund bureaucracies, and unstable national economies. But with patience and a long-term perspective, Zambia's ADMADE program may yet prove to be an "imperfect" solution in the real world of Africa.

Epilogue

Since 1989, ADMADE has undergone a dramatic, critical, and risky expansion after receiving a major grant from USAID. With this expansion, ADMADE became Zambian national policy, and the community-based approach was applied in all 32 GMAs. Yet many successful small-scale projects fail when institutional capacity is unable to keep pace with rapid expansion (Yudelman 1991), and ADMADE has not escaped such growing pains. Difficulties relate particularly to administration and political weakness in the capital and at NPWS headquarters in Chilanga, while activities in the field have continued to struggle forward slowly.

As feared, a large influx of donor funds led the department to neglect the lesson of living within its means. Desperately needed vehicles were obtained from donations, but it proved beyond the ability of wildlife-generated revenues to fund replacements. Despite the fact that vehicles were not well maintained and occasionally misappropriated, the training of unit leaders and village scouts had a demonstrable impact on poaching. The process of decentralization of wildlife decision making has continued, although abuses by some local leaders persist. ADMADE is experimening with land-use planning through a program linking traditional leaders with the technical and senior staff of NPWS. This has broken down some of the barriers of distrust between rural communities and the central government agency.

Relationships have deteriorated between the Zambian-led NPWS and the white-dominated safari hunting industry due in part to the unbusiness-like approach of the government bureaucracy. In 1993 there was a virtual collapse of safari hunting revenue, largely due to adverse publicity from former operators unhappy with the allocation of hunting areas. Zambia neither anticipated nor countered this problem with a marketing effort of its own (although that is now being corrected). Because of the sensitivity of a conservation organization working closely with an industry that many of its supporters abhorred, ADMADE and the WWF had not previously analyzed this primary source of revenue.

Relationships between the department and WWF also began to show strains over responsibility for the management of funds and program decisions. The power struggle was exacerbated by the use of expatriate consultants in the place of Zambian personnel. An external evaluation team, concerned with political problems, financial irregularities, and perhaps influenced by disgruntled safari operators, suggested that an NGO should take over management of ADMADE. This proposal was rejected by the government as a return to a colonial model of conservation.

Unless ADMADE is legally instituted, the program will be vulnerable to weak and politically motivated personnel in the Ministry of Tourism and to local residence rights issues. Abuses in the wildlife revolving fund were only addressed when the NPWS's request for an audit was backed by external donors. Civil service salaries made it impossible to compete with the private sector for key financial personnel, and regulations made it difficult to replace wardens whose performance was increasingly being compared unfavorably with that of unit leaders in the field. Recently, the problems of government staff instability turned in ADMADE's favor with the appointment of a knowledgeable and sympathetic permanent secretary in the ministry.

Low earnings from safaris and revolving-fund irregularities caused a cash flow crisis just as the approaching 1994 wet season increased prospects of renewed poaching. Showing commitment to the program, the Ministry of Finance intervened with a loan to pay village scouts, giving the program a reprieve to get its professional house in order. A reorganization under consideration gives the department greater freedom to hire and fire, set salaries, and work outside the civil service system. Despite its difficulties, ADMADE maintains the loyalty of local leaders and has slowly been providing schools, clinics, grinding mills, and jobs from natural resources. Although its future is far from assured, the program's ability to survive and adapt is encouraging.

References Cited

Anderson, David, and Richard Grove, eds. 1987. The scramble for Eden: Past, present and future in African conservation. In *Conservation in Africa: People, policies and practice* 1–12. Cambridge: Cambridge University Press.

Asibey, E. O. 1974. Wildlife as a source of protein in Africa south of the Sahara. *Biological Conservation* 6(1): 32–39.

Atkins, S. L. 1984. Socio-economic aspects of the Lupande Game Management Area. In *Proceedings of the Lupande Development Workshop*, D. B. Dalal-Clayton, ed. 49–56. Lusaka, Zambia: National Parks and Wildlife Service.

Bell, R. H. V. 1987. Conservation with a human face: Conflict and reconciliation in Africa land use planning. In *Conservation in Africa: People, policies and practice*, David Anderson and Richard Grove, eds. 79–101. Cambridge: Cambridge University Press.

Bell, R. H. V., and J. E. Clarke. 1984. Funding and financial control. In *Conservation and wildlife management in Africa*, R. V. H. Bell and E. McShane-Caluzi, eds. 545–555. Washington, D.C.: U.S. Peace Corps.

Caldecott, Julian. 1986. *Hunting and wildlife management in Sarawak*. Kuala Lumpur: World Wildlife Fund-Malaysia.

Child, Graham, and W. Nduku. 1985. Wildlife and human welfare in Zimbabwe. African Forestry Commission, United Nations Food and Agriculture Organization, 86/62, October.

Clay, Jason. 1988. Indigenous peoples and tropical forests: Models of land use and management from Latin America. *Cultural Survival Quarterly* 11–14.

Clay, Jason, ed. 1985. Parks and people. *Cultural Survival Quarterly* 9(1).

Cumming, D. H. M. 1987. A project proposal for a field study of multi-species indigenous wildlife utilization. World Wildlife Fund Project No. 3749, August.

Cumming, D. H. M., and R. D. Taylor. 1989. Identification of wildlife utilization projects for the Department of Wildlife and Parks, Government of Botswana. Gaborone: World Wildlife Fund and Kalahari Conservation Society.

Deihl, Colin. 1988. Wildlife and the Maasai: The story of East African parks. *Cultural Survival Quarterly* 9(1): 37–40.

Development Alternatives. 1989. Regional natural resources management project: Community-based resource utilization. Project paper submitted to United States Agency for International Development/Zimbabwe, August.

Gardner, J. E., and J. G. Nelson. 1981. National parks and native peoples in Northern Canada, Alaska and Northern Australia. *Environmental Conservation* 8(3).

Hancock, G. 1989. *Lords of poverty*. New York: Atlantic Monthly Press.

Hart, J. A., and G. A. Petrides. 1987. A study of relationships between Mbuti hunting systems and faunal resources in the Ituri Forest of Zaire. In *People and the tropical forest*, A. Lugo, ed. 12–14. Washington, D.C.: U.S. Department of State.

Hitchcock, R. 1989. Indigenous peoples and wildlife schemes. *Kalahari Conservation Society Newsletter* 24: 10–11.

Hopcraft, D. 1986. Wildlife land use: A realistic alternative. In *Wildlife/livestock interfaces on rangelands.* S. MacMillian, ed. 93–101. Nairobi: Winrock International.

Hunter, Malcom L., Robert K. Hitchcock, and Barbara Wyckoff-Baird. 1990. Women and wildlife in Southern Africa. *Conservation Biology* 4(4): 448–51.

International Union for the Conservation of Nature. 1981. The importance and values of wild plants and animals in Africa. Gland, Switzerland: International Union for Conservation of Nature and Natural Resources/World Wildlife Fund/ United Nations Environment Programme.

Kapungwe, E., and D. M. Lewis. 1989. Wildlife utilization schemes for local people in a wildland: A proposal submitted to Africare. October.

Lawson, N. 1985. Where whitemen come to play. *Cultural Survival Quarterly* 9(1): 54–56.

Lewis, Dale. 1989. A promise worth keeping. *Animal Kingdom* (May/June): 58–63.

Lewis, D., G. Kaweche, and A. Mwenya. 1990. Wildlife conservation outside protected areas: Lessons from an experiment in Zambia. *Conservation Biology* 4(2): 171–180.

Luangwa Integrated Resource Development Project. 1987. The Luangwa Integrated Resource Development Project: A brief description. Government of Zambia. Unpublished report.

Malama, G. 1984. Address In *Proceedings of Lupande Development Workshop.* Washington, D.C.: National Parks and Wildlife Service.

Marks, Stewart A. 1984. *The imperial lion: Human dimensions of wildlife management in Central Africa.* Boulder: Westview Press.

Matowanyika, Joseph Zans Zvapera. 1989. Cast out of Eden: Peasants versus wildlife policy in savanna Africa. *Alternatives* 16(1): 30–39.

Muir, Kay. 1988. The potential role of indigenous resources in the economic development of the arid environment in Sub-Saharan Africa. Department of Agricultural Economics and Extension Working Papers, Harare, Zimbabwe. Department of Agricultural Economics and Extension.

Murphree, M. W., and L. C. Murombedzi. 1987. Wildlife management schemes for Zimbabwe's communal areas: A preliminary survey of issues and potential sites. Centre for Applied Social Science, University of Zimbabwe, May 10.

Ntiamoa-Baidu, Yaa. 1987. West African wildlife: A resource in jeopardy. *Unasylua* 39(2).

Owen-Smith, G., and M. Jacobsohn. 1989. Involving a local community in wildlife conservation: A pilot project at Purros Southwest Kaokoland, SWA/ Namibia. *Quagga* 27: 21–28.

Parkipuny, M. S., and D. J. Berger. 1993. Sustainable utilization and management of resources in the Maasai Rangelands: The links between social justice and wildlife conservation. In *Voices from Africa*. Dale Lewis and Nick Carter, eds. Washington, D.C.: World Wildlife Fund.

Partridge, W. L. *Community and environmental rehabilitation in involuntary resettlement* (in press).

Poole, Peter. 1989. Developing a partnership of indigenous peoples, conservationists and land use planners in Latin America. In *World Bank policy, planning and research working papers*. 23–26 April.

Redford, K. H., and J. Robinson. 1987. The game of choice: Patterns of Indian and colonist hunting in the neotropics. *American Anthropologist* 89(3): 650–667.

Selpapitso, Kgosi. 1988. Legal aspects: The traditional view. In *Sustainable wildlife utilization: The role of wildlife management areas*. Gaborone, Botswana: Kalahari Conservation Society.

Turnbull, Colin M. 1972. *The mountain people*. New York: Simon and Schuster.

Volkman, Toby Alice. 1986. The hunter-gatherer myth in Southern Africa: Preserving nature or culture? *Cultural Survival Quarterly* 10(2): 25–32.

Ward, Haskell G. 1989. *African development reconsidered: New perspectives from the continent*. New York: Phelps-Stokes Institute.

Wright, Michael. 1988. People-centered conservation: An introduction. *World Wildlife Fund Letter* 3.

Yudelman, Monty. 1991. The Sasakawa-Global 2000 Project in Ghana: An evaluation. March.

CHAPTER TWO

RETHINKING CONSERVATION: THE CASE OF RANGE
MANAGEMENT

Jere L. Gilles

Many of the authors who contributed to this volume argue that the conservation of protected areas will inevitably fail if the people living in and around
these areas are not actively involved. Local populations can undermine the best-
designed conservation plans if they do not participate in their creation. In addition,
these populations often possess ecological knowledge needed by resource planners. While social scientists have long advocated including local populations in all
development efforts, this idea has not been applied easily. Today it is clear that
simply listening to local people's ideas is not enough. Technicians and biologists
also must change how they look at the world and practice their professions before
they can incorporate local people into their programs. The case of range management in lesser developed countries (LDCs) illustrates this point particularly well.

The Range Management Experience

The decades of the 1970s and 1980s were difficult for range managers
and other livestock development experts. At least 80 percent of the world's rangeland had been degraded by that time (Perry 1978), and governments and international development agencies were curtailing investments in pastoral development,
ending many programs begun in the early 1970s. This reduction and elimination
stemmed from the failure of livestock experts and range managers to devise programs that improve and protect the productivity of rangelands in LDCs.

Effective range management is the key to any successful livestock development program. However, range management specialists have been unable to
manage pastures in LDCs. The problems of pastoral development programs have
been so pervasive that even experienced range scientists have begun to question
the applicability of their "art and science" to the problems of LDCs (Greenwood
1986).

The persistent failure of pastoral development programs has generated
considerable research on the problems of pastoral development and range management. These efforts have provided a clearer understanding of livestock pro-

duction systems in developing countries and of the shortcomings of rangeland development projects. However, they have not produced an alternative approach to pastoral development. In fact, an unintended consequence of this research has been to convince investors that it is impossible to have a successful range-based livestock program in most LDCs.

Government Range Management Efforts

Long before the establishment of modern governments in much of the developing world, grazing lands were collectively controlled, and private ownership of pastureland was rare. This is in contrast to North America and Australia, where government ownership of rangelands predated its use by pastoralists, and the government's right to manage these lands was clearly recognized. As national governments in LDCs became stronger, however, they either recognized traditional land rights or imposed new land-tenure systems. Often they recognized traditional-use rights to some lands while declaring large tracts of forests and rangeland public domain. Government range managers thus faced a situation quite different from that encountered in developed nations. If traditional land-tenure systems were respected, range managers lacked legal authority to develop management plans; however, if range managers had the authority to manage rangelands as part of the public domain, they faced opposition from herders who saw their traditional rights being usurped.

The experiences of early range managers in Eastern and Southern Africa typify many of the problems range managers have encountered in LDCs. Colonial officials in these regions identified overstocking as a serious problem early in this century and introduced programs to protect rangelands and modernize livestock production (Evans 1936; Campbell 1981). As a result, they initiated destocking campaigns and encouraged pasture rotation systems.

In some ways, colonial range management efforts were similar to those in North America. Government technicians determined stocking rates and grazing patterns and required livestock owners to follow their directives. Colonial technicians, like their early U.S. counterparts, designed management programs without having a detailed understanding of rangeland ecology. There were, however, two significant differences between colonial and U.S. range management efforts. First, U.S. range managers were often stockmen themselves (who shared the values and culture of the ranchers they regulated), while colonial officers shared neither a culture nor a common definition of "overgrazing" with pastoralists. Second, U.S. ranchers had the power to modify or veto range management plans, while colonial officials strictly imposed their definition of the livestock problem on native populations and exercised considerable power over government technicians. To make matters worse, scientists had not carried out systematic research on rangeland ecology in Africa and thus were unable to provide officials with better management tools.

During the 1960s, when most African nations became independent, the United Nations Development Programme (UNDP) and the United States Agency for International Development (USAID) supported pastoral-development programs throughout the developing world (Sandford 1982). In Africa, these agencies supported the continuation and extension of range management efforts undertaken by colonial authorities. Governments forced herders to accept new management systems in the hope that once the benefits of modern husbandry techniques were demonstrated, pastoralists would eagerly adopt the new practices. Most of the programs failed, however, because pastoralists did not support them and did not believe that overgrazing and overstocking were serious problems (Moris 1986). For example, officials in the Samburu region of Kenya were able to effectively control stocking rates and improve pastures, but once the local population received authority over land use, the programs were abandoned (Campbell 1981).

In response to these failures to manage pastures by decree, governments in the 1970s attempted to give pastoralists responsibility for the rangeland they normally grazed by promoting the creation of group ranches and livestock cooperatives. Generally, group ranch membership was open to those who formerly used the land that would fall within the boundaries of a ranch cooperative. The goal of the group ranches was "to divide up the range into ecologically viable units while protecting the land rights of a majority of the pastoralists" (Oxby 1982). In some cases only a minority of grazers could participate, while in others membership was open to all herders. Livestock was individually owned within group ranches, and there was a mixture of individual and group ownership within cooperatives.

In many nations, pastoralists quickly accepted group ranches and livestock cooperatives. Membership in a group ranch or a cooperative protected pastures from incursions by farmers, secured the access of members to pastures, and made members eligible for veterinary services and development funds. However, group ranches and cooperatives turned out to be an ineffective range management tool. Members rarely adopted modern range management techniques and often did not confine their animals to the group ranch or cooperative. This led to a widespread re-examination of pastoral policies in the late 1980s.

Lessons Learned from Pastoral-Development Programs

A better understanding of pastoral-production systems now tells us why herders did not adopt modern range management practices. In particular, there are three reasons these programs failed: inadequate technical knowledge, lack of government resources, and lack of local participation in program management (Little 1982).

Comparison of Livestock Production Systems

Protein Production (kg/year)

Region	Per Hectare	Per Man-hour
United States	0.3 to 0.5	0.9 to 1.4
Australia	0.4	1.9
Sahel nomadic production	0.4	0.01
Transhumant production	0.6 to 3.2	0.01 to 0.07

Table 2.1. Livestock production on the Sahel (West Africa) and two comparable regions (adapted from Breman and de Wit 1983).

Inadequate Knowledge

Pastoral-development projects were designed to increase the production of meat and fiber by introducing modern production techniques. While livestock experts had little knowledge about the ecology of rangelands in LDCs, they knew that animal productivity on modern ranches was much higher than that of traditionally managed herds and that well-managed, Western-style ranches (Fig. 2.1) could produce twice as much meat per cow and nearly twice as much income per hectare (Pratt and Gwynne 1977; Gulbrandsen 1980). The differences in productivity were so large that planners felt little need to invest scarce funds in research. They felt that the advantages of Western ranching techniques were self-evident and that pastoralists in developing countries would eagerly agree to confine the animals to fenced pastures, to destock the ranges, and to apply pasture management techniques.

However, contrary to expectations, livestock producers usually refused to adopt the Western ranching model. While they were open to using modern veterinary practices, they refused to alter stocking rates or grazing patterns (Aboud 1982). Initially, livestock experts believed that resistance to their recommendations resulted from outmoded cultural values, and planners believed that extension projects designed to demonstrate the superiority of Western techniques would overcome pastoralist resistance. Their programs, however, failed to demonstrate the need to alter traditional herding systems. Moreover, it turned out that livestock experts had grossly underestimated the productivity of traditional production practices. One reason lies in the fact that commercial ranches specialize in the production of meat and/or fiber, while traditional herders also rely on their animals for milk and draft power. In the West, most dairy production is confined to cool, humid regions and to large-scale operations. Dairy farms do not exist in arid rangelands in LDCs, and humans must essentially compete with calves for milk. Higher calf mortality rates in traditionally managed herds reflect this competition. By not including milk consumed by humans, comparisons of calf or meat production between modern ranches and traditional production systems undervalue the productivity of the latter. If the value of milk is included in a comparative study of returns to ranches and traditional herds, traditional herders may actually produce more animal products per hectare of rangeland than do modern ranchers.

The emphasis that Western-trained agricultural scientists place on protein production *per animal* has also exaggerated the productivity of Western-style ranches. Traditional herds tend to have a larger number of small, less productive animals than do Western ranches. A 500-kilogram ranch cow may be more than twice as productive as a nomad's 250-kilogram cow, but its productive advantage diminishes when it is compared with *two* 250-kilogram cows. Some traditional systems actually produce more animal protein per hectare than U.S. and Australian ranches. For example, Table 2.1 shows that traditional West African production systems may actually outperform ranches in North America and Australia in animal protein produced per hectare (Breman and de Wit 1983; Sandford 1983). The failure to understand traditional livestock production systems, along with attempts to introduce inappropriate methods, has seriously damaged the credibility of livestock extension officers. The need for more research on animal production in LDCs is now widely recognized.

If lack of information were the only barrier to successful livestock development programs, large investments in research could easily overcome this problem. Unfortunately, the lack of adequate human and financial resources is also a major impediment to rangeland management. It takes large numbers of trained people and considerable amounts of money to organize and enforce grazing regulations, and the governments of developing countries have not had the resources to implement and to maintain such programs (Little 1982).

The history of Kenyan livestock development programs illustrates how lack of resources can frustrate range management efforts. Kenya has given a higher priority to range management than have most developing nations. Its government has a Range Management Division staffed by extension officers who work at the national, provincial, district, and local levels. Foreign governments and international agencies have provided considerable support for range management efforts, and Kenyan colleges and universities offer relevant degree programs. Kenya is also the site of several international research projects on pastoral ecology (Lusigi 1984).

Nonetheless, Kenya's programs have been hampered by insufficient resources. To begin with, there are far too few range management agents to reach the nation's pastoralists. In addition, lack of adequate transport has hampered extension programs. At times as many as 75 percent of the range service's vehicles have been incapacitated due to lack of parts, and the remaining vehicles have often stood idle because of fuel shortages (Axinn et al. 1979; Aboud 1982). Under such circumstances, it is virtually impossible for the government to initiate and to maintain grazing systems over vast stretches of rangeland. Similarly, governments throughout the developing world lack the resources to implement range management programs, and they are too poor to maintain pastoral programs initiated by foreign donors. Unless a project creates enough additional government revenue to directly pay for its year-to-year operations, it is likely to be abandoned once foreign-assistance funds are withdrawn.

Lack of Participation

Success is more likely if livestock producers are active participants in a pastoral-development plan (Ndagala 1985). Stockmen in developing countries possess practical knowledge about their production systems that can be used in the absence of scientific research, and costs to governments can be substantially reduced if livestock producers take responsibility for managing their own rangelands.

Unfortunately, U.S. and Australian range managers have had little experience or training in working with livestock producers. Extension and community organization have not been part of range management curricula, as these are not considered important skills for working on government lands in North America and Australia. Furthermore, while the U.S. government has been managing rangeland for more than 85 years, extension programs for rangeland were only begun in the last 35 years. And although the importance of extension is now recognized, it is still not the major emphasis of any range science department in the world today.

For the most part, livestock producers in the industrialized West do not participate in the initial design of grazing schemes on public lands. Preliminary design is a technical exercise carried out by government personnel. However, livestock producers can reject or amend the management plans proposed by technicians. Advisory boards, an appeal process, and the influence of legislators limit the ability of technicians to design programs that are unacceptable to livestock producers' interests. The political influence of livestock producers in North America and Australia has often been so large that government policies have often favored livestock producers at the expense of other groups (Voigt 1976; Fairweather 1982).

In contrast, political participation in rural areas of LDCs is generally low, and pastoralists usually participate even less than do other rural groups. Pastoralists typically belong to ethnic minorities who do not have good government support, and they live in remote areas far from the centers where government officials reside. Often they cannot amend resource management plans created by their governments and foreign donors. Moreover, few government range management officers are from pastoral groups, and most simply do not have the training needed to work with herders to design grazing schemes.

Problems with Western Range Management

Many development agencies have concluded that the barriers to livestock development in LDCs are insurmountable: even if enough knowledge were available to plan viable pastoral-development projects, governments lack the means to undertake them. It is also unlikely that the planning process can be decentralized so that pastoralists will have the amount of power and influence needed to actively participate in designing government programs.

Figure 2.1. A "Western"-style livestock open-range operation.

Nonetheless, one should not conclude that range management programs are impossible under such circumstances. Swiss villagers, Moroccan herders, and Fulani pastoralists have all successfully managed their pastures for centuries without the benefit of scientific research or government support (Gilles 1982). The experience of these groups and the range management principles they use can provide a model for those who wish to improve range conditions and livestock production in LDCs.

Optimal livestock and range management requires the application of a number of techniques simultaneously. These include: stocking the range with the proper kinds of animals; balancing numbers of animals with forage resources;

grazing at the correct season of year; and obtaining proper distribution of live-stock over the range (Stoddart et al. 1975). While successful indigenous range management systems emphasize the regulation of grazing seasons, trained range managers tend to focus on balancing numbers of animals.

It is primarily this Western emphasis on stocking rates that has caused the failure of range management programs in Asia, Africa, and Latin America. Before range managers develop grazing systems, they conduct an inventory of range conditions and trends. The inventory is then used to determine the grazing capacity of a pasture and the appropriate stocking rates (Klemmedson et al. 1984). Stocking rates are set so that the number of animals using a pasture does not exceed its grazing capacity, i.e., the maximum number of animals that can graze on a range without damaging forages or the soil (Stoddart et al. 1975). This concept is easy to understand. It would not be rational for livestock producers to exceed a rangeland's grazing capacity and destroy the land that supports their herds.

However, it is difficult to define or estimate the grazing capacity of a pasture, because it is not a constant value. Western scientific methods for estimating grazing capacity and stocking rates tend to yield results much lower than the "true" grazing capacity of an area (Stoddart et al. 1975). Range managers in North America and Australia have redefined grazing capacity to be a constant (the number of animals that can use land without overgrazing in all but extreme drought years) and range management texts recommend that grazing capacities and stocking rates be calculated on the basis of 65 to 80 percent of the average annual forage production (Stoddart et al. 1975). While this approach leads to an underutilization of forage resources in most years, range managers argue that any imbalance between animals and plants should favor plants, because plants are ultimately the source of sustenance for animals (Stoddart et al. 1975).

These conservative techniques waste so much forage that they have little credibility with livestock producers in LDCs, who would prefer to balance live-stock numbers with *available* forages. Nomadic and transhumant pastoralists frequently can achieve this goal by moving their animals to new pastures (see Figure 2.2), and even settled producers try to balance livestock numbers and available feed. It is not surprising that livestock producers in developing countries are slow to accept recommendations from Western range managers, especially since the recommended stocking rates are often far below the known capacity of the range (Sandford 1982).

Another problem is that even wealthy governments are unable to vary stocking rates on an annual basis, and such a strategy would be impossible for governments of LDCs. To make matters worse, the cost of conventional Western methods of determining grazing capacity is beyond the means of LDCs. Nor is there enough information about pastoral systems or about current land use patterns and animal numbers to implement relevant programs. Without more resources,

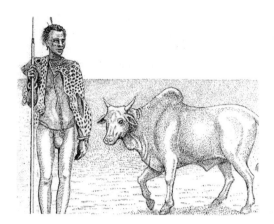

Figure 2.2. An East African pastoralist tends cattle.

it is probably impossible for LDCs to manage ranges by controlling stocking rates (Artz 1986; Fry and McCabe 1986). Fortunately, there are proven alternatives to this approach.

An Alternative Approach: Seasonal Use

In some areas of the developing world, livestock producers have developed inexpensive but effective pasture management systems by regulating season of use rather than controlling stocking rates. The persistence of these systems over centuries demonstrates that it is possible to protect and improve LDC rangelands under present conditions. Examples of well-managed systems include the "dina" system in Mali (Cisse 1986), the "agdal" system in North Africa (Gilles et al. 1986), the "hema" system in the Near East (Eighmy and Ghanem 1982; Draz 1983), and the Baluchi system of grazing reserves in Pakistan (Buzdar 1984). None of these systems emphasizes the control of stocking rates. Instead, pastures are regularly closed to grazing for a period of time to allow for renewal. In most cases, rules also govern access to pastures; these are generally flexible and may vary according to the availability of forage.

This emphasis on controlling grazing seasons eliminates some of the problems range managers have encountered in the developing world. To begin with, pasture deferment or grazing reserve systems are easier to design and manage than stock reduction programs. Pastoralists are mobile and hard to locate, they are unwilling to tell government agents how many animals they own, and groups in conflict may try to use allocation of grazing rights as a weapon against each other. Even when grazing rights are assigned, enforcing stocking regulations is difficult and expensive. In contrast, controlling the time when a pasture is used is a simpler and less expensive method. The approach requires a less detailed range inventory because it does not rely on an accurate estimate of grazing capacity, and local knowledge of forage species can be used to design these systems. Complete enumerations of livestock producers and animal numbers are not needed to establish opening and closing dates for a grazing unit, and enforcement of regulations is also simple because violation is readily observed. Furthermore, literacy and enumerative skill are not required by this form of management.

The grazing season approach has been used successfully by many government livestock development programs. For example, the government of Syria has revived the traditional "hema" grazing reserve system and has used it as the foundation of its livestock development programs (Draz 1983). Although this approach is not in itself a solution to all the problems of livestock development, it is the best approach available under current conditions. These examples indicate that by placing emphasis on the creation of grazing reserves or deferral systems, it is at least possible to arrest the deterioration of rangelands in LDCs.

Conclusion: Implications for Range Management

Social scientists have insisted that successful conservation programs must be in harmony with local culture. However, conservation techniques and procedures now applied in developing countries are a product of Western culture. The traditional range management systems discussed in this chapter apply a different set of principles than those used by university-trained conservationists. Thus, understanding local cultures will not lead to better conservation *unless* resource planners are willing to re-evaluate their own approaches and consider alternatives. By manipulating season of use rather than stocking rates, for example, range managers can avoid conflicts over the definition of grazing capacity and can develop plans that are adapted to current pastoral-production systems.

It is alarming that the failure of range management programs in LDCs has led governments and international development agencies to abandon the pastoral sector. The main explanation for these failures is that range technicians have been trying to manage pasture resources themselves and have insisted on mechanically transferring Western techniques to the developing world. If development agencies change their philosophy and place more emphasis on assisting herding groups to create self-managed pasture deferment and rotation systems— rather than focusing on overstocking—protecting and improving rangelands may still be an attainable goal.

Epilogue

In 1988 I argued that including local people in the resource management process would not by itself protect pastoral ecosystems. The assumption and theories held by professional range managers and conservationists were at odds with traditional management practices and prevented the meaningful inclusion of local populations in resource-management efforts. Because indigenous range management systems were frequently more successful than professionally managed systems in the developing world, I urged range managers and environmentalists to closely re-examine their assumptions and theories so they might better reflect the experiences of pastoralists.

By 1990 ecologists had begun to question the principles underlying modern range management (Ellis and Swift 1988; Westoby et al. 1989). These authors demonstrated that Western concepts of carrying capacity and stocking rates do not apply to many of the world's arid and semi-arid tropical regions. The notions of equilibrium, plant succession, and grazing management—the key concepts of modern Western range management—were derived from Clements' (1916) studies of Nebraska prairies (Stoddart et al. 1975). We now know that some semi-arid and arid ecosystems are almost never at equilibrium and that manipulating the stocking rates in these zones does not have a large impact on ecosystem viability.

Ecosystems in which plant and animal populations are not at equilibrium are the norm in the pastoral zones of Australia and Africa (Behnke et al. 1993) and are also common wherever biomass production varies sharply from year to year (Scoones 1994). In these systems, the grazing pressures and stocking rates recommended by modern range managers may actually lead to the deterioration of the environment (Westoby et al. 1989). Furthermore, reducing grazing pressure may not lead to improvement of rangelands, and in some cases, very heavy grazing may actually be ecologically desirable. In many areas of Africa, for example, the negative impact of overgrazing has been slight, and most damage can be traced to exceptionally dry years.

In the late 1980s my argument against the recommendations of Western range scientists was pragmatic. I felt the failure rate of range management projects in the developing world warranted the examination of alternative approaches. At the time I did not realize that there was no scientific basis for most developing world rangeland conservation projects. It is now generally accepted that the ecology of African rangelands is substantially different from that of the North American Great Plains. Readers wishing to have a concise description of current ecological thinking in this area should refer to *Range Ecology at Disequilibrium* (Behnke et al. 1993).

The challenge for conservationists today is to develop methods and institutions that reflect our new understanding of rangeland ecology. Unfortunately, until recently professional conservationists in rangeland areas used techniques largely based upon the principles outlined by Clements 75 years ago. Relatively little work has been done in this area, and much more is needed.

Currently our understanding of pastoral ecosystems in the developing world comes from the beliefs of pastoralists. Because the pastoralists could never explain their management practices in ways that Western-trained resource managers could fully understand, we have experienced more than 50 years of failed "professionally managed" pastoral-development projects. Hundreds of millions of dollars and the careers of countless dedicated professionals were wasted because "we knew better." Now we know that we did not truly understand. If range professionals had listened to local people, there would have been, at worst, no pastoral-development programs and money could have been invested in education, health care, or on otherwise improving the lives of pastoralists and the quality of the environment.

References Cited

Aboud, A. A. 1982. Range management extension services on pastoral societies in Kenya. Master's thesis. Columbus: Ohio State University.

Artz, N. E. 1986. The development implications of heterogeneity in a traditional Moroccan pastoral system: The social-technical interface. Ph.D. dissertation. Logan: Utah State University.

Axinn, G. H., J. W. Birkhead, and A. W. Sudholt. 1979. *Evaluation of the Kenya Range and Ranch Development Project.* USAID Project No. 615–0157. Nairobi: United States Agency for International Development.

Behnke, R. H., I. Scoones, and C. Kerven, eds. 1993. *Range ecology at disequilibrium: New models of natural variability and pastoral adaptation for African savannahs.* London: The Commonwealth Secretariat, Overseas Development Institute, and the International Institute for Environment and Development.

Breman, H., and C. T. de Wit. 1983. Rangeland productivity and exploitation in the Sahel. *Science* 221: 1341–1347.

Buzdar, N. 1984. Common property rights and resource use problems in Baluchistan, Pakistan. *Development Anthropology Network* 2: 12–16.

Campbell, D. J. 1981. Land-use competition at the margins of rangelands: An issue in development strategies for semi-arid areas. In *Planning African development*, G. Norcliffe and T. Penfold, eds. 39–61. London: Croom Held Ltd.

Cisse, S. 1986. Les territoires pastoraux du delta interieur du Niger. *Nomadic Peoples* 20: 21–30.

Clements, F. 1916. *Plant succession: An analysis of the development of vegetation.* Washington, D.C.: Carnegie Institution.

Draz, O. 1983. The Syrian Arab Republic: Rangeland conservation and development. *World Animal Review* 47: 2–14.

Eighmy, J. L., and Y. S. Ghanem. 1982. Prospects for traditional subsistence systems in the Arabian peninsula. *Culture and Agriculture* 16: 10–15.

Ellis, J. E. and D. M. Swift. 1988. Stability of African pastoral systems: Alternative paradigms and implications for development. *Journal of Range Management*, 41: 450–459.

Evans, P. I. B. 1936. Pasture research in the Union of South Africa. In *Pastures and forage crops in South Africa,* Bulletin No. 18, 7–8. Herbage Publication Series. Aberystwyth, Wales (U.K.): Imperial Bureau of Plant Genetics.

Fairweather, J. R. 1982. Land, state and agricultural capitalism in New Zealand: A study of change from estate to small farm production. Ph.D. dissertation. Columbia: University of Missouri.

Fry, P. H., and J. T. McCabe. 1986. *A comparison of two survey methods on pastoral Turkana migration and the implications for development planning.* Pastoral Development Network. London: Overseas Development Institute, Agricultural Administration Unit.

Gilles, J. L. 1982. Organizing for pastoral development: Themes from traditional systems. *Agriculture Administration* 11: 215–225.

Gilles, J. L., A. Hammoudi, and M. Mahdi. 1986. A high mountain agdal. In *Proceedings of the conference on common property resource management*, April 21–26, 1985, Oukaimedene, Morocco. 281–304, Conference on Common Property Resource Management. Washington, D.C.: National Academy Press.

Greenwood, G. B. 1986. Does Sahelian pastoral development include range management? _Rangelands_ 8: 259–264.

Gulbrandsen, O. 1980. A_gro-pastoral production and communal land use: A socioeconomic study of the Bangwaketse._ Bergen, Norway; Gaborone, Botswana: University of Bergen; Rural Sociology Unit, Ministry of Agriculture.

Klemmedson, J. O., M. Hironaka, and B. S. Low. 1984. Inventory of rangeland resources: Summary and recommendations. In _Developing strategies for rangeland management_, National Research Council, Committee on Developing Strategies for Rangeland Management. pp. 571–592, Boulder, Colo.: Westview Press.

Little, P. 1982. _The Workshop on Development and African Pastoral Livestock Development._ Binghamton, N.Y.: Institute for Development Anthropology.

Lusigi, W. J. 1984. Integrated assessment and management plan for western Marsabit District, northern Kenya. Integrated Project on Arid Lands Technical Report #A-6. Nairobi: United Nations Educational, Scientific and Cultural Organization-International Coordinating Council for the Programme on Man and the Biosphere (UNESCO-FRG-MAB) Integrated Project on Arid Lands.

Moris, J. 1986. _Directions in pastoral development._ Pastoral Development Network. London: Overseas Development Institute, Agricultural Administration Unit.

Ndagala, D. K. 1985. Local participation in development decisions: An introduction. _Nomadic Peoples_, 18: 3–6.

Oxby, C. 1982. Group ranches in Africa. _World Animal Review_ 42: 11–18.

Perry, R. A. 1978. Rangeland resources: Worldwide opportunities and challenges. In _Proceedings of the First International Rangeland Congress_, D.N. Hyder, ed. 7–9. Denver, Colo.: Society of Range Management.

Pratt, D. J., and M. D. Gwynne. 1977. _Rangeland management and ecology in East Africa._ London: Hodder and Stoughton.

Sandford, S. 1982. Pastoral strategies and desertification: Opportunism and con-servation in dry lands. In *Desertification and development: Dryland ecology in social perspective*, Brian Spooner and H. S. Mann, eds. 61–80. London: Academic Press.

Sandford, S. 1983. *Management of pastoral development in the Third World*. New York: John Wiley and Sons.

Scoones, I. 1994. *Living with uncertainty: New directions for pastoral develop-ment in Africa*. London: Intermediate Technology Publications., Ltd.

Stoddart, L. A., A. D. Smith, and T. W. Box. 1975. *Range management*. Third edition. New York: McGraw-Hill.

Voigt, W., Jr. 1976. *Public grazing lands: Use and misuse by industry and gov-ernment*. New Brunswick, N. J.: Rutgers University Press.

Westoby, M., B. Walker, and I. Noy-Meir. 1989. Opportunistic management for rangelands not at equilibrium. *Journal of Range Management* 43: 266–274.

CHAPTER THREE

THE CULTURAL BASIS FOR WILDLIFE CONSERVATION IN
SRI LANKA

Rasanayagam Rudran

For more than 2,000 years, Buddhism has flourished as the predominant religious philosophy of the people of Sri Lanka and has strongly influenced the country's attitudes toward nature. Today, 69 percent of the population practices Buddhism, 15 percent are Hindus and the remainder follow either Islam or Christianity (Department of Census and Statistics of Sri Lanka 1987) (see Figure 3.1).

Because Buddhism arose from Hinduism, they share several philosophical underpinnings, one of which is a deep-rooted reverence for wild animals. The elephant, for example, is identified with Lord Ganesh in the holy books of the Hindus, while other mammals, birds, and reptiles are sanctified by their association with the Hindu pantheon of gods. Likewise, the *jataka* stories of the Buddhists associate numerous animals with Gautama Buddha's life through a series of reincarnations that occurred prior to his enlightenment (Cowell et al. 1907). Rebirth, a central tenet of both religions, instills the idea that the lives of humans and animals are intimately related and that wildlife should be treated with respect.

Throughout Sri Lanka's history, several kings have enacted laws to protect wild animals. Nissanka Malla, for example, who ruled in A.D. 12, created a wildlife sanctuary just outside the ancient capital of Anuradhapura (Zuber and Bandaranaike 1979). Today, these long-held cultural beliefs continue to have a strong influence on wildlife conservation in Sri Lanka.

The Cultural Heritage of Sri Lanka

While many animals are given special respect by the Buddhist and Hindu cultures, none is as revered as the elephant. The Buddhists of Sri Lanka use the elephant to signify high social status; in ancient times, riding this animal was a royal prerogative. Former Buddhist kings declared all wild elephants their personal property and used domesticated ones as vehicles in war (Knox 1681). According to the *Mahavamsa*, which chronicles the earliest recorded history of Sri Lanka, the use of elephants in battle dates back to at least 2 B.C. (Geiger 1950). Nearly 18 centuries later, a king of Sri Lanka is reputed to have sent an army with

37

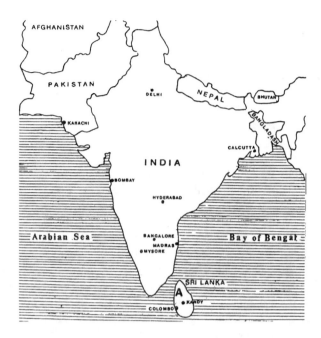

Figure 3.1. Sri Lanka (A) is an independent island country just off the southeast tip of India. Its land surface covers 25,300 square miles.

2,200 elephants to fight the Portuguese (Nicholas 1954). In order to capture, train, and care for so many animals as well as use them in trade, the former kings maintained a large state agency. Inevitably this agency served to institutionalize the elephant traditions of Sri Lanka under royal patronage. It survived as an important institution throughout the Portuguese, Dutch, and part of the British occupations of the country and was not dismantled until the early 19th century. This long history of the relationship between elephants and humans in Sri Lanka is also chronicled in numerous documents by medieval scholars regarding the care and maintenance of elephants (De Alwis 1983). Although this relationship is less evident today, the elephant is still viewed as a quasi-religious symbol of prestige, a beast of burden, and an important accessory in the cultural ceremonies of Buddhists and Hindus.

In addition to elephants and other animals, several plants are sacred to both Buddhists and Hindus. For instance, both religions regard the banyan (*Ficus religiosa*) as a holy tree (Kabilsingh 1987). In fact, the banyan under which Gautama Buddha attained enlightenment still survives in Sri Lanka as the oldest tree in the world, and it is one of the most sacred Buddhist symbols. Twenty other tree species under which earlier buddhas achieved sainthood are also highly revered (de Silva 1954). The traditional medical practice of *Ayurveda* uses remedies derived from more than 500 different indigenous plant species (Roberts 1931; Fernando 1982; Ekanayake 1984). In ancient times, these plants were tended with great care in the palace gardens of Sri Lankan kings, and the practice of herbal medicine was considered a noble pursuit restricted to kings and learned scholars such as Buddhist priests and high-caste Hindus.

This respect for animals and plants during Sri Lanka's early history was accompanied by a recognition of humankind's ability to destroy the natural environment. For example, Gautama Buddha, who spent many years in the forest, preached to his disciples that "the forest is a peculiar organism of unlimited kindness and benevolence that makes no demands for its sustenance and extends generously the products of its life activity; it affords protection to all beings, offering shade even to the axeman who destroys it" (De Rosayro 1959). Guatama Buddha prohibited the felling of trees and also regulated the use of all plant parts exploited by people for food and other purposes (Kabilsingh 1987). This concept of regulated or sustainable use of forests was further reinforced by the ancient folklore of Sri Lanka. For example, it was believed that a person lost in the forest could find plentiful sustenance in the sacred grove of the god Saman, but if he took more than he could eat, he would not find his way out of the forest (de Silva 1954). In addition, certain forest trees of large dimensions were believed to be the abodes of different gods (Fernando 1983). Consequently, the culture of Sri Lanka greatly venerated the forest and created taboos against entering it in an unclean state of mind or body (Baker 1954).

Current Status of Wildlife in Sri Lanka

Despite the close link between forests, wild animals, and the culture of Sri Lanka, the future survival of the country's wildlife has become a matter of great concern. The decline of wild animal populations and their habitats that began with colonialism was particularly evident during the British occupation from 1795 to 1948. Throughout this time, the extensive trading in elephants and ivory that occurred during the Portuguese and Dutch periods was replaced by forest clearing and sport hunting as the major threats to Sri Lanka's wildlife. Forests were cleared in the central highlands and southwestern lowlands to cultivate commercially valuable crops such as coffee, tea, rubber, and cocoa (Pakeman 1964; Anon. 1978). Beyond clearing forests, the British paid rewards for eliminating animals that raided crops. This practice led to the destruction of 5,500 elephants in less than a decade (Tennent 1863). By the end of British rule, all three Sri Lankan monkey species and several small mammals, birds, and reptiles had substantially declined in numbers (Phillips 1957).

Still, forest clearing during British occupation pales in comparison with the destruction that took place after Sri Lanka's independence. Rampant deforestation occurred as a result of the country's rapidly changing natural, social, and economic environments. While 0.8 percent of the land lost its natural cover during the last 50 years of British rule, 21.5 percent of Sri Lanka had been deforested in just three decades after independence (Andrews 1961; Anon. 1978). Most of this forest was lost to slash-and-burn agriculture as a progressively larger proportion of the country's population was forced into marginal forms of existence. Combined with the relatively slow rate of regeneration of tropical forests, this trend led to a rapid decline of forest cover throughout Sri Lanka (Richards 1952; Struhsaker 1978).

Economic-development schemes launched by the government to increase employment opportunities and agricultural productivity have also exacted a toll on Sri Lanka's forests, natural grasslands, marshes, and mangroves (Cramer 1979). For example, the ongoing two billion dollar Accelerated Mahaweli Development Program, designed to produce hydro-electric power and irrigate newly developed agricultural lands, is expected to affect the survival of several hundred elephants (De Alwis 1978; Tippetts et al. 1980). Faunal surveys indicate that this program may also have detrimental effects on 41 endemic vertebrates, including eight species of fish, two amphibians, 18 reptiles, eight birds, and three mammals (Rudran 1990). Moreover, the development area includes three endemic plant genera and at least 53 endemic plant species, 17 of which are considered rare (Cramer 1977; Kostermanns 1979). These endemic plants as well as 31 other species valuable to Western and Ayurvedic medicine are expected to decline as a result of habitat alteration within the development area (Tippetts et al. 1980).

Conservation Action: The March for Conservation

The economic-development schemes and rampant slash-and-burn agriculture that followed independence were major deviations from the environmentally conscious culture of ancient Sri Lanka. Nevertheless, the people easily accepted them in the name of increased employment and economic growth when wildlife resources were relatively abundant.

During the late 1970s, however, several individuals began voicing concerns about rapidly declining wildlife resources and the effect deforestation could have on the country's agricultural and cash-crop economy (Cramer 1977; Hoffmann 1977; Gunatilleke 1978; Perera 1978a, 1978b; Karunatilleke 1979; Tippetts et al. 1980; Santiapillai et al. 1982). As a result, the federal government took steps to address widespread environmental destruction. One of its earliest decisions was to terminate an agricultural project that for years had been degrading the natural grasslands of Horton Plains in the central highlands. Another stopped the logging of Sinharajah, which, at 9,000 hectares, is the largest patch of undisturbed rain forest left in Sri Lanka. The government then turned its attention to the Accelerated Mahaweli Development Program, which resulted in a reforestation project to rehabilitate the eroded Mahaweli River catchment, as well as the establishment of four new national parks around the area slated for development, thereby increasing Sri Lanka's protected areas by about 10 percent (Tippetts et al. 1980, 1981). The government also initiated a project in 1984 to address the wildlife problems of the Mahaweli program, and it decreed that all future development projects should be preceded by environmental impact assessments.

As the government took action to protect the environment, several people and private organizations perceived an opportunity to reverse the trend of wildlife destruction. In 1980, these interests established the March for Conservation (with financial support from foreign and local institutions) to promote wildlife conservation among all segments of the population. While the majority of the population is rural and remains steeped in ancient traditions, many rural people who depend on subsistence slash-and-burn agriculture are unaware of their impact on wildlife habitats. The March for Conservation therefore relied on long-standing, positive cultural perceptions of animals as a central theme for promoting conservation. Because current information on wildlife populations was necessary to convince decision makers, scientific research became an essential component of the program. Scientists gathered field information from localities where wildlife faced serious threats (like the Mahaweli Development Area and the Sinharajah Forest) and these data were integrated with cultural information to continue the public-education projects that had proven effective during the first year of the program.

Of the projects conducted during the first year, the one with the greatest visual impact was a colorful conservation parade that made its way through the busy streets of the capital to the sound of traditional music. The parade covered a nine-mile route and was accompanied by a very large and vocal group of adults and schoolchildren. They carried posters created by the schoolchildren that highlighted both field information and the cultural basis for wildlife conservation. Within days of the parade, all major newspapers of Sri Lanka ran editorial columns strongly supporting the message conveyed to the public, and the parade is now repeated annually in urban and rural towns with the active participation of governmental and nongovernmental organizations.

Another public-education project that became a regular feature was a school lecture program on wildlife conservation topics. Because high school teachers are poorly informed about native species and environments and students are sometimes tested on these subjects at public examinations, the lecture program was a great success. Over the years, lecture topics have changed, attendance has increased, and awards for conservation quizzes, essays, and poster contests have helped maintain school children's interest. Exhibitions on local wildlife and ecosystems that proved popular with the public were also repeated regularly. Like other public-education projects, these exhibitions included little-known social and scientific facts illustrating the benefits of wildlife conservation. In all these projects, organizers attracted media coverage by giving local dignitaries a prominent role.

The March for Conservation thus carried its message to the public both directly through its education projects and indirectly via newspapers, radio, and television. Moreover, by conducting several projects each year, the program has been able to keep wildlife conservation constantly alive in the minds of the public.

In addition to public-education projects, the March for Conservation organized scientific seminars to lobby the country's decision makers. At a seminar on the Sinharajah Forest, for example, scientists presented their findings on the detrimental effects of deforestation on the forest's rich endemic fauna. These discussions (as well as information provided by others) provided compelling reasons for protecting the Sinharajah (Senanayake et al. 1977; Gunatilleke 1978; Hoffmann 1979; Gunatilleke and Gunatilleke 1981; Rudran 1982; Kotagama and Karunaratne 1983). In 1984, the Sinharajah was declared an International Man and Biosphere Reserve, and the March for Conservation continues to make its presence felt there through an expanded research program. Field data showing the negative impact of the Mahaweli Development Program on endemic fauna and flora have also contributed to the establishment of four national parks.

While the organizers of the March for Conservation adopted a mixed strategy to promote wildlife awareness, others initiated programs with mainly a cultural focus. A Buddhist priest, for instance, began a successful and much publicized tree-planting campaign based on the Buddhist doctrine. Similarly, a Hindu businessman used his cultural traditions to promote planting of trees in the country's arid north, where Hindus predominate. In another example, a practitioner of Western medicine used social traditions to protect sea turtles that nested near a village along the west coast. In this case, women's traditional role as the principal homemakers in Sri Lankan society helped prevent the consumption of turtle eggs and meat, especially by men at the local tavern.

These individual efforts, as well as the March for Conservation program, illustrate that cultural values still play an important role in promoting a conservation ethic in Sri Lanka, and they are the most frequent basis for the actions of committed conservationists. Yet, compared with the seriousness of the conservation problem, all of these efforts are relatively limited in scope due to the financial constraints of individuals and nongovernmental organizations. To increase the impact of conservation, the government should also incorporate cultural values in its programs to promote wildlife conservation.

Elephant Conservation in Sri Lanka

An opportunity to incorporate cultural values into a government conservation program arose with the initiation of the Mahaweli Environment Project in 1984. In that project, the U.S. Agency for International Development funded a team of U.S. National Park Service and Smithsonian personnel to provide techni-

Figure 3.2. A Sri Lankan mahout works his elephant. Trained elephants provide labor that is cheap, efficient, and practical in rural areas throughout Sri Lanka.

cal assistance on various environmental issues such as public education, park planning, and wildlife management. With regard to wildlife management, the elephant proved to be the species of greatest concern. Once quite numerous throughout the island, elephants had become restricted to the dry zone where they came into conflict with humans—especially with farmers who had colonized recently established agricultural lands. Colonist farmers, without using traditional methods of guarding their crops and property, cast aside cultural sentiments and frequently opened fire at crop-raiding elephants (Poulier 1955; Anon. 1959). As the elephant population dwindled to only a few thousand, the Accelerated Mahaweli Development Program threatened to increase elephant mortality even further (McKay 1973; Hoffmann 1975, 1978; Olivier 1978).

Given the endangered status of the elephant and its historic social value in Sri Lanka, a strategy incorporating aspects of culture as well as scientific research was necessary to conserve and manage this species. In 1985, the U.S. Technical Assistance Team proposed such a strategy, which included three integrated programs. The first dealt with managing elephants in their natural habitats, particularly in the national parks established around the Mahaweli Development Area. The program included ecological research and habitat management within the national parks, the elimination of wounded elephants that had turned hostile towards humans, and the construction of physical barriers to prevent animals from leaving the parks and entering the development area.

The second program addressed the plight of elephants that already lived within the development area and were therefore in conflict with agriculturists. To mitigate this conflict and the loss of agricultural revenue, the program recommended capturing elephants, partly for the purpose of domestication. This recommendation was based on local demand for tame elephants, whose numbers had declined by about 35 percent since 1970 (Jayasinghe and Jainudeen 1970; De Alwis 1982). In addition, three other options were recommended for elephants captured by the government. The first option was to translocate elephants to protected areas where the animals were known to occur below carrying capacity; the second was to establish a government-run center for maintaining captives, especially for breeding purposes and training as work elephants (Figure 3.2); and the third was to sell selected captives at public auctions and use the proceeds to pay communities that had been hurt by elephant depredations. This last option was intended to get farming communities to consider the monetary value of elephants and refrain from shooting crop raiders, which undoubtedly would make elephant capture less hazardous and perhaps more successful. The termination of shooting, however, greatly depended on the willingness of communities to support the elephant capture operations. Because public cooperation was necessary to implement various aspects of elephant capture, an outreach program was developed to solicit community cooperation by publicizing a proposed new option of compensating farmers with proceeds of elephant auctions.

Another important objective of the outreach program was to promote the revival of traditional methods of guarding crops against elephants. For centuries, the use of fences, fires, drums, and the vigilance of entire communities had proved effective in preventing elephants from entering agricultural areas (Poulier 1955). This method was successfully employed by long-established communities that had evolved strong social traditions of mutual assistance and voluntary community service. Lacking social integration, the more recently formed colonist communities no longer practiced these methods. The outreach program proposed a plan to rally the colonists around the problem of elephant depredations, thereby hastening the social integration of the new community. The plan's success depended on convincing colonists who lived near the center of the agricultural area that farmers at the periphery (who sustained most of the crop damage) were likely to abandon their farms unless assisted. Peripheral abandonment would cause increased crop damage in the central areas, a prediction intended to encourage the entire community to guard the periphery. To substantiate the need for crop guarding, the plan called for documentation of crop damage areas in colonist communities. In addition, the outreach program included public-education projects similar to those conducted by the March for Conservation.

Since 1985, the government has taken some steps to implement the proposed strategy for the conservation and management of elephants. People have been recruited and sent abroad for training in modern methods of elephant capture and control, preparations have been made for the construction of an Elephant Management Center, surveys have been initiated to identify problematic herds and the areas of crop damage, and public-education projects have been conducted in the Mahaweli Development Area. However, much work remains before these efforts to conserve and manage elephants and other wildlife in Sri Lanka can be declared a success.

Conclusion

The Sri Lankan experience demonstrates that cultural arguments appeal only to those with strong social traditions and must be strengthened by arguments based on science in order to be truly effective in promoting wildlife conservation. In Sri Lanka, as in many other tropical countries, there are very few people who are qualified to conduct scientific research on fauna and flora. In the future, training in scientific research will be just as important as using cultural traditions in public-education projects to promote wildlife conservation in the tropics.

Epilogue

Since the late 1980s, the Sri Lankan government has taken some important steps to help conserve the country's wildlife. In 1988, for example, it unveiled a comprehensive national conservation strategy designed to promote the sustainable use of natural resources. Two years later, this strategy was used to develop the country's first-ever national policy on wildlife conservation. In response to these government actions, the U.S. Agency for International Development and other donor agencies have committed more than U.S.$5 million to environmental conservation in Sri Lanka.

The government used some of these much-needed funds to conduct a biodiversity survey and inventory focusing on the flora of the country's Wet Zone. It has also made a few attempts to address human-elephant conflicts and the conservation of Sri Lanka's most endangered animal species. However, because the country still has no coherent wildlife conservation plan, most funds earmarked for faunal conservation remain unused nearly three years after they were allocated. This problem is particularly evident in the country's efforts to conserve the elephant (Rudran et al. in press). Nevertheless, the commitment shown by the government in recent years suggests that it is likely to develop a coordinated action plan for animal conservation in the near future.

The task of promoting wildlife conservation in a densely populated and relatively poor country such as Sri Lanka is bound to be challenging. The task is made even more difficult by the country's decade-long ethnic conflict, which has been a major distraction to the people and the government. Despite these problems, Sri Lankans still cherish the cultural values that have enabled them to share a small island with large animals for many centuries. The fact that they are more keenly aware than ever before of the need to conserve their environment and wildlife gives reason to be optimistic about future prospects for conservation in Sri Lanka.

References Cited

Andrews, J. 1961. *A forestry inventory of Ceylon*. A Canada-Colombo plan project. Colombo, Ceylon: Government Press.

Anon. 1959. Report of the Committee on Preservation of Wildlife. Sessional paper. Colombo: Government Press.

Anon. 1978. Forests: Their role in human welfare and economic value. *Economic Review* 3: 3–15. (A publication of the People's Bank of Sri Lanka.)

Baker, J. 1954. The Sinharajah rainforest, Ceylon. *Geographical Journal* 89: 539–551.

Cowell, E., R. Chalmers, W. Rouse, M. Francis, and A. Neill, eds. 1907. *The Jataka*, or *Stories of the Buddha's former births* (1978 reprint). New Delhi: Cosmo Publications.

Cramer, L. 1977. The significance of the indigenous flora in the area of the Mahaweli complex. S*ri Lanka Forester* 13: 9–18.

Cramer, L. 1979. The natural environment. *Vidurava* 4: 15–21. Colombo: National Science Council of Sri Lanka.

De Alwis, W. 1978. The future of wildlife populations in the Lower Mahaweli Region. Unpublished document of the Department of Wildlife Conservation, Colombo, Sri Lanka.

De Alwis, W. 1982. *Census of domesticated elephants and tuskers in Sri Lanka*. Colombo: Department of Wildlife Conservation.

De Alwis, W. 1983. *Let them live*. Colombo: Department of Wildlife Conservation.

Department of Census and Statistics of Sri Lanka. 1987. *Statistical pocket book of Sri Lanka*. Colombo: Department of Government Publications.

De Rosayro, R. A. 1959. Editorial notes. *The Ceylon Forester* 4: 99–102.

de Silva, W. 1954. A contribution to Sinhalese plant lore. *The Ceylon Forester* 1: 89–102.

Ekanayake, D. 1984. Important medicinal plant components of the Sri Lanka flora. *Loris* 16: 276–280.

Environmental assessment: Excelerated Mahweli Development Program. 1980. Colombo, Ceylon: Tippetts, Abbett, McCarthy, Stratton, Inc.

Environmental assessment: Excelerated Mahweli Development Program. 1981. Colombo, Ceylon: Tippetts, Abbett, McCarthy, Stratton, Inc.

Fernando, S. 1982. *Herbal food and medicines in Sri Lanka*. Colombo: The National NGO Council of Sri Lanka.

Fernando, S. 1983. Indigenous medicine and herbal plants. *Loris* 15: 288–290.

Geiger, W. 1950. *The Mahavamsa*. Colombo: Ceylon Government Information Department.

Gunatilleke, C. V. S. 1978. Sinharajah today. *The Sri Lanka Forester* 13: 57–64.

Gunatilleke, C. V. S. and I. A. U. N. Gunatilleke. 1981. The floristic composition of Sinharajah: A rainforest in Sri Lanka with special reference to endemics and dipterocarps. *The Malaysian Forester* 44: 386–396.

Hoffmann, T. 1975. Elephants in Sri Lanka: Their number and distribution. *Loris* 13: 278–280.

Hoffmann, T. 1977. Major threat to oldest wildlife reserve. *Loris* 14: 133–137.

Hoffmann, T. 1978. Distribution of elephants in Sri Lanka. *Loris* 14: 366–367.

Hoffmann, T. 1979. The forest of the lion king. *Animal Kingdom* 82: 23–30.

Jayasinghe, J., and M. Jainudeen. 1970. A census of the tame elephant population in Ceylon with reference to location and distribution. *Ceylon Journal of Science* 8: 63–68.

Kabilsingh, C. 1987. How Buddhism can help protect nature. In *Tree of life: Buddhism and the protection of nature*, S. Davies, ed. 7–16. Bangkok: Buddhist Perception of Nature.

Karunatilleke, H. 1979. The fruitless exploitation of Sinharajah. *Vidurava* 4: 4–7.

Knox, R. 1681. *An historical relation of the island Ceylon in the East Indies.* Reprinted 1958. Colombo, Sri Lanka: Tisara Prakasakyo.

Kostermanns, A. 1979. Endemic plants of the Accelerated Mahaweli Development Program Area. Report presented at the Workshop on Endemic Species and the Accelerated Mahaweli Development Program held at the National Museum, Colombo, Sri Lanka, November 1979.

Kotagama, S. W., and P. B. Karunaratne. 1983. Checklist of the mammals (Mammalia) of the Sinharajah MAB reserve. *The Sri Lanka Forester* 16: 29–35.

McKay, G. 1973. Behavior and ecology of the Asiatic elephant in southeastern Ceylon. *Smithsonian Contributions to Zoology* 125: 1–113.

Nicholas, C. 1954. From the warden's field book (Part II): The Ceylon elephant in antiquity. *The Ceylon Forester* 1: 103–111.

Olivier, R. 1978. Distribution and status of the Asian elephant. *Oryx* 14: 380–424.

Pakeman, S. 1964. *Ceylon.* New York: Frederick A. Praeger.

Perera, W. R. H. 1978a. Catchment areas and the protection of environment. *The Sri Lanka Forester* 13: 49–51.

Perera, W. R. H. 1978b. Thotapolakanda: An environmental disaster? *The Sri Lanka Forester* 13: 53–56.

Phillips, W. W. A. 1957. A survey of the more recent changes in the status and distribution of the wildlife of Ceylon. In Sir Paul Pieris Felicitation, Sir Paul Pieris Felicitation Volume Committee, ed. 83–99. Colombo: The Apothecatie Company Ltd.

Poulier, R. S. V. 1955. Protection of crops against wild elephants. *The Ceylon Forester* 2: 34–37.

Richards, R. 1952. *The tropical rainforest: An ecological study.* Cambridge: Cambridge University Press.

Roberts, E. 1931. V*egetable materia medica of India and Ceylon.* Colombo: Plate Ltd.

Rudran, R. 1982. Effects of deforestation on the endemic species of Sinharajah forest, Sri Lanka. In *World Wildlife Fund Yearbook,* 105–107. Gland, Switzerland: World Wildlife Fund.

Rudran, R. 1990. Problems and prospects for wildlife conservation in Sri Lanka. In *Conservation in developing countries: Problems and prospects.Proceedings of the Centenary Seminar of the Bombay Natural History Society,* J. C. Daniel and J. S. Serrao, eds. pp. 252–259. Oxford: Oxford University Press.

Rudran, R., J. Jayewardene, and W.A. Jayasinghe. In press. Need for an integrated approach to elephant conservation in Sri Lanka. In *Proceedings of the International Seminar on the Conservation of the Asian Elephant,* J.C. Daniel, ed. Bombay: Bombay Natural History Society.

Santiapillai, C., M. R. Chambers, and N. Ishwaran. 1982. The leopard in the Ruhuna National Park, Sri Lanka, and observations relevant to its conservation. *Biological Conservation* 23: 5–14.

Senanayake, F., M. Soulé, and J. Senner. 1977. Habitat values and endemicity in the vanishing rainforests of Sri Lanka. *Nature* 265: 351–354.

Struhsaker, T. 1978. Bioeconomic reasons for conserving tropical rainforests. In *Recent advances in primatology,* Vol. 2, D. J. Chivers and W. Lane-Petter, eds. London: Academic Press.

Tennent, E. 1863. *The natural history of Ceylon.* London: Longmans Green.

Zuber, C., and S. Bandaranaike. 1979. *Sri Lanka: Island civilization.* Colombo: Lake House Book Shop.

CHAPTER FOUR

NATIONAL RECREATION AREAS IN APPALACHIA: CITIZEN PARTICIPATION IN PLANNING AND MANAGEMENT

Benita J. Howell

After almost three decades of special federal attention, Appalachia is still one of the least developed regions of the United States, compared by political economists to the former colonies of industrial nations. With respect to land use and resource planning, many of the political, economic, and social issues that now complicate conservation in Appalachia run parallel to those in lesser-developed nations, especially regarding the relationships among land management agencies and local people.

Historical Perspective

In the United States, the 1960s were marked by both intensified international development efforts and by a domestic "War on Poverty" that included many programs in Appalachia. At the same time the War on Poverty brought Appalachia's economic plight into the national media spotlight, environmentalists began organizing to combat irresponsible exploitation of natural resources, particularly cut-and-run timbering and strip mining. This increased public concern for the environment—particularly in stopping further abuse, reclaiming land, and restoring water quality—was accompanied by an increasing demand for outdoor recreation among residents of the highly urbanized eastern seaboard.

In 1962, a new kind of land management unit, the National Recreation Area (NRA), was established to conserve natural areas not given national park status. NRAs were located within 250-mile driving distances of major cities, providing for outdoor recreation needs more fully than federal lands set aside solely for conservation or managed for multiple extractive uses. Soon after, the Land and Water Conservation Act (LWCA) of 1965 provided funding for land acquisition by federal, state, and local agencies, with the stipulation that 85 percent of the funds be spent to acquire lands in the eastern part of the country. Geographically, Appalachia was well situated to take advantage of the new NRA program and to seek LWCA funds to acquire land for that purpose (Fitch and Shanklin 1970; Douglass 1975).

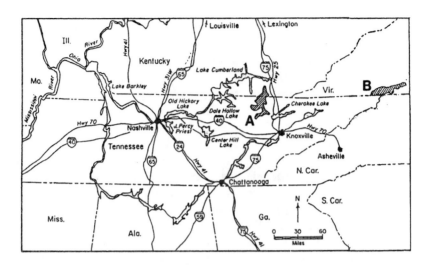

Figure 4.1. Big South Fork National Recreation Area is located on the south fork of the Cumberland River on the border between Kentucky and Tennessee (A). Mount Rogers National Recreation Area is located in the southwesternmost part of Virginia along the Tennessee/North Carolina border (B).

Further encouragement came from the Appalachia Regional Commission (ARC), a federally funded consortium of Appalachian state governors that advocated tourism and recreation as a means of economic development in isolated rural areas (Walp 1970).

Two of the new NRAs established in Appalachia (Figure 4.1) are Mount Rogers in southwest Virginia (authorized in 1966) and Big South Fork in eastern Kentucky and Tennessee (authorized in 1974). Congress directed that the Big South Fork project be planned and constructed by the U.S. Army Corps of Engineers (COE) but managed by the National Park Service (NPS). In contrast, the Mount Rogers NRA was developed by the U.S. Forest Service as a unit of the existing Jefferson National Forest.

From the beginning, both projects had multiple, potentially conflicting goals: to conserve and, in the case of Big South Fork, to rehabilitate distinctive natural areas; to provide outdoor recreation facilities; and to stimulate local economies by generating tourism. The conflicting goals of resource conservation and tourism divided NRA planners and local people in both projects. However, the outcomes in the two cases were quite different. While public groups have become effectively involved in co-managing resources at Mount Rogers over the past 20 years, the Big South Fork project has essentially failed to achieve significant public involvement. Because of underlying similarities in the plans initially drawn up for the two recreation areas and the similar issues that these plans raised, the two cases permit an informative comparison of planning and management procedures used by different federal land-management agencies, particularly their openness to citizen participation.

Both cases illustrate the critical role agency organization and local culture play in the design and, especially, implementation of public-participation programs. In any agency, historically important missions, legislative mandates, and organizational structure are reflected in agency values and procedures. These elements of institutional culture can either facilitate or undermine public involvement in resource management decisions. Because institutional culture has this power to shape behavior, some land management agencies may require substantial reform before they can hope to turn their co-management rhetoric into action.

The Big South Fork NRA

The Big South Fork area is located on the Cumberland Plateau in one of the less mountainous sections of Appalachia. A gorge along the Big South Fork of the Cumberland River forms the scenic centerpiece of this 123,000-acre area, which combines both National River and National Recreation Area designations. Visitors can enjoy whitewater rafting and canoeing, fishing and hunting, and 200 miles of hiking and equestrian trails. Visitor centers, campgrounds, and a coal-mining museum have been built, and two lodges are planned, one in Kentucky and the other in Tennessee.

From the 1880s to the 1960s, local leaders and their congressional delegations made periodic efforts to secure a hydroelectric dam on the Big South Fork. They hoped that manufacturing might replace timber and coal industries that had languished since the 1930s (Howell 1981). From 1967 to 1968, however, Tennessee environmentalists successfully lobbied Congress to consider the possibility of leaving the Big South Fork a free-flowing stream, hoping to develop the area's recreation potential while preserving and, where necessary, reclaiming its natural and scenic assets. Despite the beauty of the river gorge, mining and clearcutting had produced serious erosion and water pollution. Abandoned farmsteads, railroads, and industrial sites dotted the landscape; neglected country roads had become tracks for off-road vehicles bringing groups from nearby towns to hunt, fish, camp, and carouse. The lobbying efforts of environmentalists ultimately led to the authorization of the Big South Fork National River and Recreation Area in 1974. Given the long history of project proposals for the region, many local people felt that Congress had made this decision almost overnight and more in response to outsiders' desires than to local needs for more jobs (see a description of local opposition in Howell 1984).

Planning for the Big South Fork National River and Recreation Area was complex, yet it failed to adequately involve citizen participation. COE was responsible for planning, acquiring land, and constructing facilities, while NPS was responsible for managing the area. This meant that planning was in the hands of an agency with no permanent management role in the project, and NPS, despite its long-term stake in resource management, had only a secondary advisory role in planning. NPS also had a very modest budget compared with the millions of dollars controlled by COE. In addition, an interim land management agreement between these agencies placed uniformed Park Service rangers in the area as soon as sufficient land had been obtained to require their presence. This situation only confused the public further because the federal agents most visible to them had little responsibility for critical planning decisions such as boundary determination.

Members of the public found that gaining access to the appropriate people to ask questions or state opinions was a confusing process. COE, for example, handled assessment and land acquisition in-house, but its planning branch contracted with private firms for the environmental assessment and master plan. Numerous contractors and subcontractors from government agencies, private firms, and universities were responsible for various aspects of the project, from research on natural and cultural resources to the design of interpretive exhibits. In addition, COE planners coordinated contractors' work out of the Nashville district office and made periodic site visits to the Big South Fork area. However, tightly scheduled site visit itineraries did not permit sufficient time and opportunity for project managers to evaluate local conditions and interact with a broad representative sample of citizens. Project managers and contractors established contact with various federal, state, and local agencies as well as political and business leaders, but no attempt was made to incorporate broadly based input from local people in the master plan.

In addition to the many agencies involved in planning and management, the Big South Fork Preservation Coalition was created by the Tennessee Citizens for Wilderness Planning in conjunction with other environmental and historic-preservation groups. The group presented its position paper to COE in mid-1975 when the Corps' earliest planning documents were still in preparation. The coalition's position paper identified resource conservation as the primary goal of the NRA, an intent that required low-impact, low-density, nonmotorized forms of recreation. The coalition further recommended that lodge construction have low priority and that lodges be small, rustic buildings with minimal visual and vehicular impact on their surroundings. It also recommended closing many existing unpaved roads and prohibiting off-road vehicles throughout the area. Although the coalition observed that land acquisition was the most pressing priority to prevent impending harm to resources and to minimize costs, its position paper recommended that five areas of plateau farmland and residences be excluded from the project boundaries. Because these tracts were not essential to project goals, it was felt that if they were acquired by pressure tactics, they would likely focus suspicion and hostility toward the Big South Fork NRA.

A draft environmental impact statement was transmitted to the Council on Environmental Quality in October 1975. Responses from various environmental groups reiterated the coalition's earlier advocacy of minimal development within the boundaries and again stated the need for the proposed boundaries to be modified. Although these comments were published in an addendum to the Final Environmental Impact Statement (U.S. Army Corps of Engineers 1976a), controversial issues were not discussed in the body of that document. The General Design Memorandum, published by COE concurrently with the environmental impact statement, opted for the most intensive level of development (U.S. Army Corps of Engineers 1976b). However, the memorandum did not acknowledge the controversial nature of this decision.

While environmentalists were frustrated by their apparent failure to communicate effectively with planners, local people responded even more emotionally to a plan that they viewed as transferring their land to outsiders, depriving them of their own favorite recreational activities, and locking up commercially valuable natural resources along with future jobs (Howell 1983, 1989). Whereas environmentalists felt that the plan called for too much development, local people saw too little development to provide the economic stimulus they wanted. Both segments of the public agreed, however, on the need to redraw boundaries to minimize unnecessary relocations of homes and farms that were outside of the environmentally sensitive river gorge area. Yet even when subsequent federal budget cuts delayed property acquisition, there was no reappraisal of whether certain upland areas ultimately should be acquired.

As predicted, COE inflexibility on this point generated considerable hostility toward the project in general. As a result, many nonresident landowners actively expressed their opposition to land acquisition and their distrust of the property valuation process by accelerating timber cutting and oil production in extremely sensitive areas near streams. By the time a draft of the master plan was presented at public meetings in 1979, the public was convinced that COE had already made final decisions regarding the appropriate balance between resource preservation and recreation goals and had determined specific means for achieving that mix without considering public opinion. As Mazmanian and Nienaber (1979) have suggested, COE used public hearings to sell their plan to the public and, if possible, override any opposition that had emerged (see also Checkoway 1981). Acting on the assumption that the Corps itself could best determine the intent of the enabling legislation and the national interest, COE viewed public participation as a forum for selling the plan to the public.

As a result, both pro-conservation and pro-development segments of the public were disillusioned with aspects of the plan that ignored their concerns, and both viewed the plan as making too many concessions to the other side. Skepticism, hostility, and bitterness resulted from the failure to include more open public participation in the planning strategy. Furthermore, these attitudes complicated efforts to restore water quality, check erosion, enhance wildlife habitat, and reforest the area. These efforts became more time consuming and more costly than originally anticipated.

Mount Rogers NRA

The Mount Rogers National Recreation Area in southwest Virginia lies between Interstate 81 and the North Carolina state line, encompassing the most rugged mountains in Virginia. Its 154,000 acres include Whitetop Mountain, Pine Mountain, and Mount Rogers (which, at 5,729 feet, is the state's highest peak). Approximately 111,000 acres are in National Forest ownership.

Unlike the Cumberland Plateau, the Blue Ridge region of Appalachia produces no coal; however, iron, zinc, lead, and manganese have all been mined there in the past. While timbering in this region has declined since World War II, it was the principal industry in the early 20th century. Logging and burning created alpine meadows that have been maintained more recently through grazing. While farming has declined in this region, farms here are better maintained and more prosperous than in the Big South Fork region, and farming has remained a viable commercial enterprise in some sections near the NRA. In addition to farming, some small communities have also attempted to expand employment opportunities by attracting light industry. These efforts have met with only limited success, however, and as a result many workers have been forced to commute long distances to work in regional centers (see U.S. Forest Service 1977a for a description of the environmental and socioeconomic background of the Mount Rogers area). Fortunately, the rural isolation in this area—coupled with outstanding scenery, wildlife, and trout streams—makes it an ideal setting for pursuing tourism and recreation as an alternative to industrial development.

Even before the Appalachian Regional Commission was created, Congressman Pat Jennings began a campaign to promote tourism in what he styled the "Whitetop Wonderland" of southwestern Virginia. The new NRA program made possible federal assistance for this endeavor, which was enthusiastically endorsed by local leaders and businessmen. With the support of the Forest Service, Congress created the Mount Rogers NRA on May 31, 1966. At that time, the Jefferson National Forest already controlled 84,000 acres of the designated area, and 70,000 acres were in private holdings.

By February 1967, local citizens had organized a seminar to discuss the NRA project and its potential economic impact. Organized as the Mount Rogers Citizens Development Corporation (MRCDC), the group wished "to insure that persons of the area [would] reap the benefits of the increased tourism that [would] bring dollars to this area, rather than having outsiders control the economic interests of the Mount Rogers area." Charles Blankenship, the planner for the Forest Service on the project, developed close contacts with this group as a means of keeping the public informed, gathering public reaction and input, and encouraging local interest in land use planning and formation of a regional planning commission (Blankenship 1987). While some members voiced concern that haphazard, unregulated development could spoil the very natural assets that would attract visitors, the local government and business interests represented in MRCDC unanimously favored development over resource conservation.

The Forest Service produced an ambitious plan in response to its congressional mandate and the aspirations of the pro-development local constituency. The plan included a 63-mile scenic highway along the Iron Mountain range that would link Interstates 77 and 81, a ski slope, a winter sports complex, a year-round resort at Whitetop Mountain, eight recreation areas for camping and picnicking, and seven impoundments for water supply and recreation purposes. Visitorship was estimated to reach one million by 1976 and five million by 2000. The Forest Service and local citizens enjoyed a solid consensus on the content and goals of the Mount Rogers plan until the Forest Service began proceedings to acquire additional acreage, some of it in holdings (private land surrounded by federal property) that local businessmen had envisioned developing privately.

In the years between the mid-sixties and the mid-seventies, the demography and social climate of southwest Virginia had changed. Significant numbers of well-educated, environmentally conscious ex-urbanites moved into the area, attracted by its rural peace and quiet. These newcomers had the will and the organizational skills to launch a campaign against what they saw as over-development, particularly the scenic highway and ski resort proposals. Controversy over land acquisition drew long-time local residents into the opposition movement (Bingham 1978; Mastran and Lowerre 1983). This new constituency found its opportunity to work constructively for a more modest, environmentally sensitive level of development at Mount Rogers, largely because the Forest Service made genuine efforts to respond to requirements for environmental assessment and public input contained in the National Environmental Policy Act.

When the 1978 Draft Plan and Environmental Impact Study (U.S. Forest Service 1978) advocated essentially the same level of development as had been envisioned in the 1969 preliminary plan, opponents who organized as Citizens for Southwest Virginia prepared a detailed response and orchestrated an effective letter-writing and petition campaign to urge modifications. The deadline for response to the Draft Plan and Environmental Impact Statement was extended from May 3, 1978, until August 4, 1978. During this time, Forest Service representatives met with civic organizations, political bodies, special-interest groups, and interested citizens. They participated in open discussions on radio and in TV interview and call-in shows, and they took bus tours of the area, including two weekend "work-

shop tours" attended by representatives of national environmental and conservation organizations (Blankenship, personal communication). They explained their
thinking on the plan but also listened to what the public had to say.

Correspondence received in response to the Draft Plan and Environmental Impact Statement was systematically catalogued, tallied, and analyzed according to general Forest Service guidelines for handling public comment (U.S. Forest
Service 1977b). Ten areas of controversy were identified, each of which was addressed in detail in the final management plan and Federal Environmental Impact
Statement (U.S. Forest Service 1978). These areas included the scenic highway,
scope and development, social and cultural change, economic growth, land acquisition, wildlife and fisheries, trails, the ski area, timber management, and administrative concerns such as law enforcement, solid-waste disposal, fire protection,
and permits.

Responses to the draft plan made it clear that, by the late seventies, there
was substantial public sentiment to limit the scope of development in order to
minimize undesirable sociocultural change and uncontrolled growth of resort and
second-home developments. Five million visitors per year seemed too many for
either local people or the Recreation Area to absorb without an adverse impact.
Much of the controversy surrounding the draft plan related specifically to a
newfound concern for natural resource conservation and a preference for low-
impact outdoor recreation over motorized, resort-style tourism. For example, environmentalists pointed out that construction of the scenic highway and the ski
resort at Whitetop would destroy the sensitive alpine meadows and subject them
to continued degradation through overuse. Trail users also objected to destruction
of the Iron Mountain Trail that already occupied the proposed highway corridor.
Both the highway and the ski resort were dropped from the final plan, as was all
mention of resort-style lodges. Trout fishermen also objected to impoundments
proposed for native trout streams. The Forest Service responded to these objec-
tions by eliminating proposed impoundments from three streams and planning
additional measures to minimize effects on fisheries caused by the remaining impoundments and by wastewater management. Opposition to timber clear-cutting
and constructing timber access roads was a relatively minor issue because of low
demand for timber in this area. A 1979 timber management plan for Jefferson
National Forest designated most of it a wilderness area; elsewhere in the NRA,
timber harvesting and grazing were geared toward enhancing and maintaining
habitat diversity and suitable conditions for wildlife.

During the 1980s, advisory committees composed of a cross-section of
the public played a substantial role from the earliest stages in developing management plans for the wilderness area. For example, each group negotiated conflicting interests in a series of workshop meetings (Grimes 1987). While tight federal
budgets during the eighties hampered rangers' ability to carry out all the desired
programs, they also had a positive side effect by encouraging citizen volunteer

programs. Horseback riders and hikers helped maintain their trails; campground users policed campgrounds; hunters took responsibility for maintaining access roads they wished to keep open; and, in the process, all learned more about the issues surrounding resource management at Mount Rogers.

Neither the pro-development leaders who boosted the Mount Rogers project in the early sixties nor the environmentalists got everything they wanted in the final plan, but each won some victories and knew that the Forest Service had given due consideration to public opinion. Furthermore, the satisfactory mediation between pro-development and environmentalist positions laid the groundwork for continuing public involvement in planning and resource management at Mount Rogers. The benefits accrued thus far include the Forest Service's increased sensitivity to environmental and related social concerns, the general public's greater understanding of resource management issues, and the growing role of citizen-volunteers as co-managers.

The Cases Compared: Critical Differences

There are four key differences in organization and structure between the Big South Fork and Mount Rogers projects. First, at Mount Rogers there was continuity of responsibility for land management and planning both before and after creation of the NRA, an advantage that did not exist at Big South Fork. Both the Corps of Engineers and the National Park Service were newcomers to the Big South Fork region, and their divided responsibilities led to confusion among citizens.

Because all planning and management personnel at Mount Rogers were associated with Jefferson National Forest, they were in a position to establish direct, effective communication between their agency and the public. In contrast, contractors from private firms or universities working at Big South Fork followed the standards of their various disciplines or professions rather than develop new COE standards for public participation. Moreover, these contractors had no long-term commitment to the project or the area.

The third difference was that the Forest Service at Mount Rogers gave greater consideration than did Big South Fork planners to what might happen or should happen outside the project boundaries. Private holdings at Mount Rogers necessitated a comprehensive approach to planning, while the elimination of all private holdings at Big South Fork made it possible for planners to focus their attention exclusively on federal lands. Contractors working on various aspects of the Big South Fork plan were not authorized to address issues of regional planning and socioeconomic development outside the recreation area boundaries, although local citizens perceived these issues as critically important.

Finally, and probably most important, the citizen participation process developed at Mount Rogers was viewed as open and fair by the public. In contrast, the citizens at Big South Fork found COE virtually unresponsive to their attempts to participate in planning. Public opinion played a small role in shaping the final plan, and conflict between conservationists and development-oriented groups predominated and strengthened the COE instinct to plan *for* the public rather than *with* it.

Conclusion

Given similar projects and local cultural environments, why did the Forest Service accommodate citizen participation more readily than did the Corps of Engineers? Like Culhane (1981), I believe the difficult task of multiple-use resource management suggests one answer. Dealing with multiple-user constituencies has created a strong incentive for the Forest Service to develop effective means to assess public opinion and negotiate compromise among conflicting interests (Hall 1963; Devall 1973; Martin 1969). History, particularly the development of core values and goals, is a key element in understanding an agency's culture. In this case, the historical association of the Forest Service with the Department of Agriculture has oriented that agency toward values and goals that are compatible with outreach to rural people (Kaufman 1960; Robinson 1975; Steen 1976; Frome 1984). Reforestation, forest conservation education, and community contact have been particularly visible Forest Service activities in Appalachia since the 1930s (see Mastran and Lowerre 1983). In a sense, these values and activities have pre-adapted Forest Service personnel to interact sensitively with rural communities whose traditional ways of life and future economic well-being must be balanced with the conservation goals of Appalachia's new National Recreation Areas.

Epilogue

Although this chapter was first written in the late 1980s, citizen involvement through volunteer programs and policy consultation has continued to be a touchstone of National Forest management. Since 1990, for example, the District Ranger for Mount Rogers NRA has sought public response to proposed actions ranging from special-use permits for harvesting fir cones and maple sap to major campground construction and trail rerouting. In addition, the master plan for the NRA is updated every five years, giving the public ample opportunity to share in defining long-range goals. (A more detailed discussion of local public reaction to the Big South Fork and Mount Rogers NRAs can be found in Howell 1990).

Meanwhile citizen involvement in the Big South Fork NRA has improved as a result of a major change in management. In 1990, Congress authorized the transfer of the area to the National Park Service, thereby ending all Corps of Engineers involvement. Formal dedication of Park Service headquarters in the summer of 1991 symbolized the beginning of what is hoped will be an era of greater harmony and collaboration between the NRA and its neighbors (Howell 1993).

The NPS has also made great progress over the past decade toward addressing cultural issues at the policy level. For example, it has expanded its definition of cultural resources and sought local expertise in response to the American Indian Religious Freedom Act, which protects sacred sites and materials, and the Native American Graves Protection and Repatriation Act (Howell 1994a; Stoffle and Evans 1994). In addition, to meet new challenges in resource management, a long-standing organizational division between cultural and natural resources is finally being bridged (Howell 1994b). Applied cultural anthropologists are now on staff in several NPS regional offices (see Ruppert 1994 for a description of their activities). Revised management policies for the park system reflect new appreciation for diverse ways of life, ethnographic research, and the traditional knowledge held by tribal elders. Officials are now drafting comparable standards for NPS professionals who consult with state and other external agencies (National Park Service 1994). These standards recognize the value of expertise in areas ranging from land use planning and community development to cultural anthropology and folklore. They also acknowledge native experts who lack the usual professional credentials. In fact, cultural considerations have gained this visibility in NPS largely because the sovereign status of recognized Indian tribes requires special measures (see Howell 1994a). One hopes these examples of cultural sensitivity will set precedents for wider ranging collaboration between all public land management agencies and neighboring communities in the near future.

References Cited

Bingham, E. 1978. The impact of recreational development on pioneer lifestyles in southern Appalachia. In *Colonialism in modern America: The Appalachian case*, H. M. Lewis, L. Johnson, and D. Askins, eds. 57–70. Boone, N.C.: Appalachian Consortium Press.

Blankenship, C. A. (N.d.) *The Mount Rogers National Recreation Area: A history of land use planning and public involvement.* Typescript on file at NRA Headquarters, Marion, Va.

Blankenship, C. A. Interview by author, July 13, 1987.

Checkoway, B. 1981. The politics of public hearings. *The Journal of Applied Behavioral Science* 17: 566–582.

Culhane, P. J. 1981. *Public lands politics: Interest group influence on the forest service and the Bureau of Land Management.* Baltimore, Md.: The Johns Hopkins University Press.

Devall, W. B. 1973. The Forest Service and its clients: Input to Forest Service decision-making. *Environmental Affairs* 2: 732–757.

Douglass, R. W. 1975. *Forest recreation.* Second Edition. New York: Pergamon Press.

Fitch, E., and J. F. Shanklin. 1970. *The bureau of outdoor recreation.* New York: Praeger Press.

Frome, M. 1984. *The Forest Service.* Second Edition. Boulder, Colo.: Westview Press.

Grimes, L. Interview by author, August 4, 1987.

Hall, G. R. 1963. The myth and reality of multiple-use forestry. *Natural Resources Journal* 3: 276–290.

Howell, B. J. 1981. A survey of folklife along the Big South Fork of the Cumberland River. Report of Investigations No. 30. Knoxville: University of Tennessee Anthropology Department.

Howell, B. J. 1983. Implications of the cultural conservation report for social impact assessment. *Human Organization* 42: 346–50.

Howell, B. J. 1984. Folklife research in environmental planning. In *Applied social science for environmental planners*, W. Millsap, ed. 127–139. Boulder, Colo.: Westview Press.

Howell, B. J. 1989. The anthropologist as advocate for local interests in national park planning. In *International perspectives on cultural parks: Proceedings of the First World Congress*, 275–280. Washington, D.C.: U.S. National Park Service and Colorado State Museum.

Howell, B. J. 1990. Mediating environmental policy conflicts in Appalachian communities. In *Environment in Appalachia*, J. W. Bagby, ed. 103–109. Lexington: University of Kentucky Appalachian Center.

Howell, B. J. 1993. Social impact assessment and cultural conservation: Implications for local public involvement in planning. In *Environmental analysis: The NEPA experience*, S. G. Hildebrand and J. B. Cannon, eds. 274–288. Boca Raton, Fl.: Lewis Publishers/CRC Press.

Howell, B. J. 1994a. Folklife, cultural conservation, and environmental planning. In *Putting folklore to use*, M. O. Jones, ed. 94–114. Lexington: University of Kentucky Press.

Howell, B. J. 1994b. Linking cultural and natural conservation in National Park Service policies and programs. In *Conserving culture: A new discourse on heritage*, M. Hufford, ed. 122–137. Urbana: University of Illinois Press.

Kaufman, H. 1960. *The forest ranger: A study in administrative behavior*. Baltimore, Md.: Johns Hopkins University Press.

Martin, P. L. 1969. Conflict resolution through the multiple-use concept in Forest Service decision-making. *Natural Resources Journal* 9: 228–236.

Mastran, S. S., and N. Lowerre. 1983. *Mountaineers and rangers: A history of federal forest management in the Southern Appalachians, 1900–1981*. Washington, D.C.: United States Department of Agriculture, Forest Service.

Mazmanian, D., and J. Nienaber. 1979. *Can organizations change? Environmental protection, citizen participation, and the Corps of Engineers*. Washington, D.C.: Brookings Institution.

National Park Service, Interagency Resources Division. 1994. Secretary of the Interior Historic Preservation Professional Qualifications Standards (draft).

Robinson, G. O. 1975. *The Forest Service: A study in public land management*. Baltimore, Md.: Johns Hopkins University Press.

Ruppert, D. 1994. Redefining relationships: American Indians and national parks. *Practicing Anthropology* 16(3): 10–13.

Steen, H. K. 1976. *The U.S. Forest Service: A history*. Seattle: University of Washington Press.

Stoffle, R. W., and M. J. Evans. 1994. To bury the ancestors: A view of NAGPRA. *Practicing Anthropology* 16(3): 29–33.

U.S. Army Corps of Engineers. 1976a. Big South Fork National River and Recreation Area final environmental impact statement. Nashville, Tenn.: U.S. Army Corps of Engineers.

U.S. Army Corps of Engineers. 1976b. Big South Fork National River and Recreation Area general design memorandum (DM No. 1). Nashville, Tenn.: U.S. Army Corps of Engineers.

U.S. Forest Service. 1977a. Mount Rogers National Recreation Area: Draft environmental statement. Washington, D.C.: U.S. Dept. of Agriculture, Forest Service.

U.S. Forest Service. 1977b. *Forest Service inform and involve handbook* (draft). Washington, D.C.: U.S. Department of Agriculture, Forest Service.

U.S. Forest Service. 1978. Mount Rogers National Recreation Area final management plan and environmental impact statement. Washington, D.C.: U.S. Department of Agriculture, Forest Service.

Walp, N. 1970. The market for recreation in the Appalachian highlands. *Appalachia* 3: 27–36.

CHAPTER FIVE

CULTURE AND THE COMMONS

Bonnie J. McCay

Since Garrett Hardin's "The Tragedy of the Commons" appeared in *Science* magazine in 1968, his ideas have been hotly debated and widely criticized. According to his model of resource use, resources held in common cannot be properly managed; for example, the additive social cost of putting one more cow in a pasture or taking one more load of fish from the sea is never recognized or considered by an individual. According to Hardin's model, even if an individual sees evidence of overgrazing or fish stock depletion and feels that something should be done to protect the sustainability of the resource, that person would be a fool to limit his or her own level of use while others continue to take more. The "tragedy of the commons" therefore lies in the supposedly inevitable reality that even when the level of demand for common resources is high enough to threaten their sustainability (through population increase, economic growth, or shifts in markets, for example), users will continue to deplete the resources.

The assumption that common property (in contrast to private property) creates a system in which individuals behave against the interests of the group is not new. For example, Aristotle remarked 2,000 years ago: "That which is common to the greatest number has the least care bestowed upon it" (Cass and Edney 1978). Hardin reiterated this idea in stating that "freedom in a commons brings ruin to all" (Hardin 1968). The tragedy-of-the-commons model has led many people to assume that resource management cannot be effective unless the resource is either privatized (so that the long-term costs and benefits of alternative uses are internalized by the users) or there is strong government intervention (in cases where scarce, mobile, and diffused resources are difficult to make private). As we witness the seemingly limited ability of humans to care for nature, Hardin's arguments that conservation problems must be addressed with changes in social institutions and morality still hold true today. However, experience has also shown that his model has flaws that must be reconsidered, particularly its failure to recognize and address the potential of social institutions in effective natural resource management.

Criticisms of the Tragedy-of-the-Commons Model

One way that Hardin's model is fundamentally flawed is its assumption that individuals have no relationship with each other beyond competition for shared and limited resources, an assumption that may be due to his incorrect interpretation of common property (Runge 1981; Kimber 1981). Hardin uses the term as a synonym for "open access resources," that is, resources from which no one can be excluded and to which no individual has specific rights. This is in sharp contrast to the definition of common property as that which belongs to the community (Hoebel 1954; Bohannan 1963; Furubotn and Pejovich 1972). Hardin failed to recognize that once there is some definition of property—even a determination that all members of a community or nation should have free and equal rights—the potential for social deliberation on the uses, management, and allocation of resources is present. For example, critics of Hardin have shown that the traditional English commons—the source of Hardin's parable—was often regulated admirably by villagers and manor courts (Cox 1985). In fact, there are many apparently viable systems of communal resource management throughout the world among hunter-gatherers, pastoralists, fishermen, and farmers (Gilles and Jamtgaard 1981; Berkes 1989; McCay and Acheson 1987). Contrary to the limiting assumptions of the "tragedy," common property encompasses a wide variety of institutional arrangements that delimit access and impose restrictions on use. Such systems manage tribal property, the communal lands of peasant communities, fishing, hunting and trapping, oil and gas exploitation, and grazing allotments on federal rangelands. By equating common property with open access, the tragedy-of-the-commons approach ignores these social institutions and their roles in managing the commons.

Hardin's policy solutions—government intervention or privatization— can actually worsen environmental degradation by weakening or demolishing existing institutions. Several studies have provided examples of how privatization worsens environmental problems (McCay and Acheson 1987; National Research Council 1986; Berkes 1989). Not only does Hardin's model simplify the importance of factors related to capitalism and other manifestations of an industrialized, complex world, but it also gives little weight to what can be considered "tragedies of the commoners:" people who depend for all or part of their livelihoods on open access to communal resources (Franke and Chasin 1980; Emmerson 1980). Social, cultural, and economic dislocations and distress may follow attempts to privatize or to impose government management. This happened during the postmedieval "enclosure" movement in many Western European countries, where land once held in common by subsistence farmers became privatized, usually by large and powerful landholders who farmed for profit (Thompson 1975; Cox 1985; Ciriacy-Wantrup and Bishop 1975). There are many other examples from around the world, past and present, of people uprooted and impoverished because of losing access to natural resources to which they once had communal rights. Not only do the former "commoners" suffer, but they also may be forced to overuse and abuse the resources they are left with or undermine the value of the management systems put into place. The persistence of poaching, for example, is often attributed to a manifestation of the need to assert common rights and rebuke imposed management efforts (McCay 1984; Howkins 1979; Thompson 1975; McCay 1987; Taylor 1981).

In contrast to Hardin's interpretation, the concept of the commons has been seen in a positive light, especially by those who hold the suspicion that "individualism" is flawed (Bloch 1930). Proponents of this philosophy often romanticize life in small rural communities where people share the very land they depend upon (Fernandez 1987). This romantic perspective is a more optimistic view of human nature than is Hardin's. It leaves open the possibility of "comedy" in an encyclopedia definition: Whether or not the story has a happy ending, it reflects "the drama of humans as social rather than private beings [as well as the] drama of social actions having a frankly corrective purpose" (Smith 1984). From this romantic perspective, the individual herdsman in Hardin's model becomes a person who is a member of a community of herders with a more or less shared interest in managing the common pasture (of course, one's perception of just what one's "share" is may be the basis of comedy, drama, or both). This romantic alternative to Hardin's gloomy assessment of the commons is flawed as well. It carries unsupported assertions about the conservation value of all "traditional" resource use systems and the behavior of all hunter-gatherers, and it assumes that these people are "natural conservers" who never use more resources than they need to survive (Bodley 1982; Boulding 1977). As with Hardin's criticisms of the commons, this tendency to romanticize human communities and their resource management abilities must be corrected by employing empirical, theoretically informed research to address questions about the conditions under which resource conservation takes place, what conservation is, and how its success can be measured (Hames 1987; Brightman 1987; Berkes 1987; Stocks 1987; Feit, this volume). The key to this task lies in appreciating the necessary interactions among local people and those who control their access to resources (Pinkerton 1987; Anderson 1987; Durrenberger and Palsson 1987).

Communal Resource Management in Canadian and U.S. Fisheries

A recent collection of ethnographic case studies of fisheries (as well as foraging, grazing, and farming commons) suggests that people can, and often do, manage communal resources and that those resources are very rarely treated as completely open access (McCay and Acheson 1987). The critical question for conservation is: "Under what conditions will people successfully manage the commons?" (McCay and Acheson 1987; Ostrom 1987; Hames 1987). Recognition that native peoples have developed systems that restrict access to and use of marine and terrestrial resources (once thought to be open access and unmanaged) has

renewed interest in the use of these traditional systems as the framework for ecologically sound economic development and socially acceptable resource management (Johannes 1981; Morauta et al., 1982; Ruddle and Akimichi 1984; Ruddle
and Johannes 1985). Moreover, understanding the cultural framework for successful communal resource management schemes is crucial to planning conservation projects. To an outsider, what may look like a system that will conserve natural
resources, such as limited or even fully privatized access, may be used in entirely
different ways and for entirely different purposes. Jim Carrier showed this in his
study of reef tenure among the Ponam islanders of Papua New Guinea (Carrier
1987; Polunin 1984). On the other hand, what may initially appear to be a system
that violates all of our notions of achieving conservation—such as Cree Indian
fishing practices studied by Fikret Berkes (1987)—may prove sustainable upon
closer examination.

Research among commercial fishermen of Canada and the eastern seaboard of the United States illustrates that it is possible to develop models of communal regulation of common-property resources that rely neither on a view of
human nature as inherently cooperative and self-denying nor on a view of it as
inherently self-serving and individualistic. Interestingly, the projects described
here were not specifically designed to conserve endangered resources. For instance, a self-regulating fishing system used by marketing cooperatives in New
Jersey was designed to optimize economic returns; in Newfoundland, institutions
allocating fishing space were designed to manage potentially divisive and costly
conflicts; and in New Jersey, New York, Maryland, and elsewhere on the eastern
seaboard of the United States, community regulations for clamming and oystering
were designed to maintain high employment by preventing the use of efficient
harvesting machines and the participation of large companies. Even a management system developed by the fishing community with state and federal governments in response to a severe decline in certain shellfish stocks is oriented more
toward economic than conservation goals. However, all these examples of communal regulation provide clues to successful conservation strategies that address
social as well as biological concerns.

Cooperatives and Catch Limits

The two fish-marketing cooperatives that were studied in New Jersey in
the late 1970s and early 1980s are small and specialized organizations established
in the early 1950s to help fishermen market their fish. Because their members rely
on the fish trade to urban markets and on middlemen and urban market wholesal-
ers, these organizations impose catch limits on members. The limits are intended
to minimize the "glut" phenomenon on the market, for when large quantities of
fish come in, all fishermen suffer from low prices. This example clearly dispels

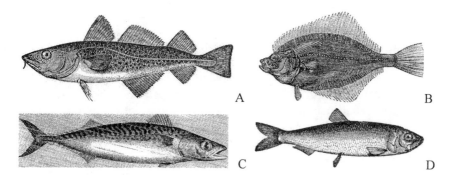

Figure 5.1. Major Atlantic Ocean food fishes of great concern to fishermen along the north-eastern coast of North America: (A) cod, (B) flounder, (C) mackerel, and (D) herring. Maintaining a "fair" distribution of access to fish species such as cod does not necessarily prevent overfishing of cod stocks.

assumptions about users of the commons as fiercely competitive and unable to agree. Moreover, in at least one of the cooperatives, catch limits are handled in sophisticated ways to both reward skill and luck and to penalize those who attempt to violate the rules (McCay 1980). These are tricks that no government system of management has yet learned. According to the fishermen interviewed, it is important but incidental that the system also helps reduce fishing pressure on some stocks (see Figure 5.1).

Fishing Space in Newfoundland

Newfoundland, like most of the Westernized world, has long been under a regime in which fishing rights are accessible to all citizens. Around the turn of this century, however, the government began to acknowledge and support the legitimacy of local systems of access management. Increased use of certain fixed-fishing gears, particularly the large cod trap, was accompanied by conflicts over places to set these traps as well as conflicts between trap fishermen and other kinds of fishermen. In response, most communities, which depend heavily on fishing, developed their own systems of regulation that established when and how people could claim trap sites and where and when the different and potentially conflicting kinds of gear could be placed (McCay 1976; Martin 1979). These rules were intended to help reduce potentially divisive and costly conflict over fishing space and resources in communities that exhibit what might be called an "egalitarian veneer" (Martin 1979). They were not intended to prevent overfishing of cod stocks, but instead to help maintain a "fair" distribution of access to cod.

Shellfishing Regulations on the Eastern Seaboard of the U.S.

In many places along the eastern seaboard, it is illegal to use anything but one's hand, toes, or crude short- and long-handled rakes to capture clams and oysters. In much of New York's shellfishing habitats and in Maryland's portion of the Chesapeake Bay, it is almost impossible for people to obtain private property or leaseholds in shellfish beds despite the logic and ease of so doing, given the work that goes into managing shellfish and the immobility of these creatures once settled into the bottom. These laws are often seen as an anachronistic outgrowth of strong Jeffersonian or "home rule" politics along the mid-Atlantic seaboard (McHugh 1972) and as obstacles to profitability and progress (Agnello and Donnelley 1975). But they continue, and their defense by shellfishermen continues. The major reason seems to be that the laws maintain employment opportunities for large numbers of people who are more or less dependent on the region's estuaries. Clammers and oystermen are well aware that more advanced technology is available, yet few have been in a financial position to invest in it. In short, the laws protect the majority against the minority. The laws also reflect beliefs that the use of more efficient technology would lead not only to "unfair" monopolization of the resources but also to their rapid depletion.

Sea Clamming, Economics, and the Commons

Sea clams are large bivalves that are processed for frozen, fried, and canned-clam products, supplying a large industry that is concentrated in the mid-Atlantic region. This industry provides an example of a system that, while enforced by the federal government, has been developed through a democratic process in which the resource users have played a key role. In 1977, when the United States followed Canada and other nations in agreeing to the establishment of a 200-mile exclusive fishing or economic zone at sea, Congress included provisions for a system to manage foreign and domestic fisheries within this 200-mile limit. Regional management councils were established, and the Mid-Atlantic Fisheries Management Council was among the first to use the new system to set management procedures for sea clams. The council established an annual quota and a moratorium on entering the fishery. Those already in the fishery were forced to keep the vessels they had or replace them, if sunk, with vessels of roughly similar capacity. Finally, participants were required to adhere to a schedule limiting the time they were permitted to fish.

No one expected the 1978 sea clam management system to endure the moratorium and restrictions on fishing time with such a strict quota. Yet the process has endured and is essentially the same today as it was before. Over the years, vessel owners have increased the effectiveness of their vessels and gear by changing the size of equipment such as dredges and hydraulic hoses. Because the quota has stayed roughly what it was in the late 1970s, this increased capacity means that vessels working four or five days a week in 1978 were working six hours every two or three weeks just a decade later!

Several factors make it remarkable that this quota system has lasted so long: a system of participatory democracy enhanced by the power of special-interest lobbyists, a tremendous build-up in catching capacity within the fleet, the cultural commitment of fishery participants to profit making, an unusual practice of keeping vessels in port except for a handful of hours every few weeks, and the fact that the clam resource itself has been spectacularly abundant in most areas. But the explanation is simple: An increased quota and/or decreased size limit would cause prices to plummet, endangering fishermen and processors alike. At the same time, the sea clammers acknowledge that they are helping preserve a limited resource.

Conclusion

Biologists and administrators concerned with conservation often deplore the fact that protecting threatened fish populations is not the primary goal of the institutions developed in fishing communities. However, to be effective in meeting conservation goals, management systems should meet some of the shorter-term economic interests of those who are managed and/or help preserve highly valued community goals. Otherwise, we may repeat what happened hundreds of years ago in the wake of the enclosure movement in the British Isles that robbed peasant farmers of their land and forced their movement into the cities to become the urban poor. It was a tragedy of the commoners, and it did not protect the commons. The examples presented here suggest that communal regulations of common-property resources exist and that they rely neither on a view of human nature as inherently cooperative and self-denying nor on a Hobbesian view of it as inherently self-serving and individualist. It is important that conservationists appreciate that fact and try to understand the structural, situational, and cultural conditions under which people will and will not cooperate to protect habitats and species that they value.

Epilogue

Since 1988, dramatic changes have intensified all of the issues discussed in the chapter. The groundfish complex of major fish stocks in the northwest Atlantic off the coasts of Newfoundland, Nova Scotia, and even New England has collapsed.

In Newfoundland, commercial fishing for cod, flounder, and other groundfish virtually ended in 1992. In other areas, it is severely restricted, with even more restrictions in sight. The species involved, the timing, the extent, and the causes of the collapse vary from one area to the other. Because they involve a combination of factors including overfishing (which itself has many causes), apparent environmental and ecological changes, scientific error, and hubris compounded by defects in the policy process, sorting out the causes of the collapse is extremely difficult. Serious attention is now being given in both the United States and Canada to alternative models of fishery management, including "co-management" and more decentralized systems that incorporate local communities.

The sea clam management system described in the chapter also changed significantly. In 1990 it became the first fishery in the United States to be managed with "individual transferable quotas" (ITQs). Canada already had some examples of similarly privatized fisheries management. In the early 1990s, both countries also became more seriously focused on the possibilities of using ITQs to help reduce participation in troubled fisheries. Conflicts between ITQs and community interests have emerged, however, highlighting the bankruptcy of approaches that do not place cultural systems at the center of public policy.

References Cited

Agnello, R. J., and L. P. Donnelley. 1975. Prices and property rights in the fisheries. *Southern Economic Journal* 42: 253–262.

Anderson, E. N., Jr. 1987. A Malaysian tragedy of the commons. In *The question of the commons*, B. McCay and J. Acheson, eds. 327–343. Tucson: University of Arizona Press.

Berkes, F. 1987. Common-property resource management and Cree Indian fisheries in subarctic Canada. In *The question of the commons*, B. McCay and J. Acheson, eds. 66–91. Tucson: University of Arizona Press.

Berkes, F. 1989. *Common property resources: Ecology of community-based sustainable development*. London: Belhaven Press.

Bloch, M. 1930. La lutte pour l'individualisme agraire dans la France de xviiie siècle. *Annales d'histoire Economique et Sociale* 11: 329–383, 511–556.

Bodley, J. H. 1982. *Victims of progress*. Palo Alto, Calif.: Mayfield Publishing Co.

Bohannan, P. 1963. Land, "tenure," and land tenure. In *Agrarian systems*, D. Biebuyk, ed. 101–115. Oxford: Oxford University Press.

Boulding, K. E. 1977. Commons and community: The idea of a public. In *Managing the commons*, G. Hardin and J. Baden, eds. San Francisco, Calif.: W. H. Freeman.

Brightman, R. A. 1987. Conservation and resource depletion: The case of the boreal forest Algonquians. In *The question of the commons*, B. McCay and J. Acheson, eds. 121–141. Tucson: University of Arizona Press.

Carrier, J. G. 1987. Marine tenure and conservation in Papua New Guinea: Problems in interpretation. In *The question of the commons*, B. McCay and J. Acheson, eds. 142–167. Tucson: University of Arizona Press.

Cass, R. C., and J. J. Edney. 1978. The commons dilemma: A simulation testing the effects of resource visibility and territorial division. *Human Ecology* 6: 371–386.

Ciriacy-Wantrup, S. W., and R. C. Bishop. 1975. "Common property" and natural resource policy. *Natural Resources Journal* 15: 713–727.

Cox, S. J. B. 1985. No tragedy on the common. *Environmental Ethics* 7: 49–61.

Durrenberger, E. P., and G. Palsson. 1987. The grassroots and the state: Resource management in Icelandic fishing. In *The question of the commons*, B. McCay and J. Acheson, eds. 370–392. Tucson: University of Arizona Press.

Emmerson, D. K. 1980. Rethinking artisanal fisheries development: Western concepts, Asian experiences. World Bank Staff Working Paper no. 423. Washington, D.C.: World Bank.

Fernandez, J. W. 1987. The call to the commons: Decline and recommitment in Asturias, Spain. In *The question of the commons*, B. McCay and J. Acheson, eds. 266–289. Tucson: University of Arizona Press.

Franke, R. W., and B. J. Chasin. 1980. *Seeds of famine: Ecological destruction and the development dilemma in the West African Sahel*. Montclair, N. J.: Allenheld Osmun.

Furubotn, E. G., and S. Pejovich. 1972. Property rights and economic theory: A survey of recent literature. *Journal of Economic Literature* 10: 1137–1162.

Gilles, J. L., and K. Jamtgaard. 1981. Overgrazing in pastoral areas: The commons reconsidered. *Sociologica Ruralus* 21: 129–141.

Hames, R. 1987. Game conservation or efficient hunting? In *The question of the commons*, B. McCay and J. Acheson, eds. 92–107. Tucson: University of Arizona Press.

Hardin, G. 1968. The tragedy of the commons. *Science* 162: 1243–1248.

Hoebel, E. A. 1954. *The law of primitive man*. Cambridge, Mass.: Harvard University Press.

Howkins, A. 1979. Economic crime and class law: Poaching and the game laws, 1840–1880. In *The imposition of law*, S. B. Burman and B. E. Harrell-Bond, eds. 273–287. New York: Academic Press.

Johannes, R. E. 1981. *Words of the lagoon: Fishing and marine lore in the Palau district of Micronesia*. Berkeley: University of California Press.

Kimber, R. 1981. Collective action and the fallacy of the liberal fallacy. *World Politics* 33: 178–196.

Martin, K. O. 1979. Play by the rules or don't play at all: Space division and resource allocation in a rural Newfoundland fishing community. In *North Atlantic maritime cultures*, R. Andersen, ed. 276–298. The Hague: Mouton.

McCay, B. J. 1976. Appropriate technology and coastal fishermen of Newfoundland. Ph.D. dissertation. New York: Columbia University.

McCay, B. J. 1980. A fishermen's cooperative, limited: Indigenous resource management in a complex society. *Anthropological Quarterly* 53: 29–38.

McCay, B. J. 1984. The pirates of Piscary: Ethnohistory of illegal fishing in New Jersey. *Ethnohistory* 31: 17–37.

McCay, B. J. 1987. The culture of the commoners: Historical observations on old and new world fisheries. In *The question of the commons*, B. McCay and J. Acheson, eds. 195–216. Tucson, Arizona: University of Arizona Press.

McCay, B. J., and J. M. Acheson, eds. 1987. *The question of the commons: The culture and ecology of communal resources*. Tucson: University of Arizona Press.

McHugh, J. L. 1972. Jeffersonian democracy and the fisheries. In *World fisheries policy*, B. J. Rothschild, ed. 134–155. Seattle: University of Washington Press.

Morauta, L., J. Pernetta, and W. Heaney, eds. 1982. *Traditional conservation in Papua New Guinea: Implications for today.* Monograph 16. Boroko, Papua New Guinea: Institute of Applied Social and Economic Research.

National Research Council. 1986. *Proceedings of the Conference on Common Property Resource Management, April 21–26, 1985.* Washington, D.C.: National Academy Press.

Ostrom, E. 1987. Institutional arrangements for resolving the commons dilemma: Some contending approaches. In *The question of the commons*, B. McCay and J. Acheson, eds. 150–165. Tucson: University of Arizona Press.

Pinkerton, E. 1987. Intercepting the state: Dramatic processes in the assertion of local co-management rights. In *The question of the commons*, B. McCay and J. Acheson, eds. 344–369. Tucson: University of Arizona Press.

Polunin, N. 1984. Do traditional marine tenure systems conserve? Indonesian and New Guinean evidence. In *Maritime institutions in the Western Pacific*. Senri Ethnological Studies, No. 17. K. Ruddle and T. Akimichi, eds. 267–283. Osaka: National Museum of Ethnology.

Ruddle, K., and T. Akimichi, eds. 1984. *Maritime institutions in the Western Pacific*. Senri Ethnological Studies, No. 17. Osaka: National Museum of Ethnology.

Ruddle, K., and R. E. Johannes, eds. 1985. *The traditional knowledge and management of coastal systems in Asia and the Pacific.* Jakarta: UNESCO Regional Office for Science and Technology for Southeast Asia.

Runge, C. F. 1981. Common property externalities: Isolation, assurance and resource depletion in a traditional grazing context. *American Journal of Agricultural Economics* 63: 595–606.

Smith, M. E. 1984. The triage of the commons. Paper presented at the annual meeting of the Society for Applied Anthropology, Toronto, Canada, March 1984.

Stocks, A. 1987. Resource management in an Amazon Varzea lake ecosystem: The Cocamilla case. In *The question of the commons*, B. McCay and J. Acheson, eds. 108–120. Tucson: University of Arizona Press.

Taylor, L. 1981. "Man the fisher": Salmon fishing and the expression of community in a rural Irish settlement. *American Ethnologist* 8: 774–788.

Thompson, E. P. 1975. *Whigs and hunters*. London: Allen Lane.

CHAPTER SIX

CONSERVATION MUST PAY

Jeffrey A. McNeely

Like many protected areas in the tropics, Thailand's Khao Yai National Park (Figure 6.1) has been plagued by encroachment and widespread poaching. In 1972 the park was in serious jeopardy, its boundaries steadily receding inward and its wildlife disappearing. So many elephants, gibbons, tigers, gaur, deer, pheasants, and hornbills fell prey to hunters' guns that only small remnants of the park's once-abundant wildlife remained. The first solution conservationists attempted was simply to enforce the law more strongly. Patrols were increased, and pitched battles with poachers resulted in bloodshed and death on both sides. This strategy failed miserably. Villagers, arguing that they had inhabited the land long before it became a park, said they needed its land and wildlife to earn a living. To them, park protection meant unjust efforts to force poor farmers to suffer and sacrifice for the benefit of rich tourists from Bangkok (Praween et al. 1988).

The problems of Khao Yai are not unique. Central governments throughout the tropics have frequently failed to conserve wildlife and wildlands through the force of law. In many cases, these efforts have been driven by far-away interests such as tourists. These outsiders have dramatically different perspectives on conservation than the farmer who watches a herd of satiated elephants retreat at dawn from his ravaged cornfield to a neighboring national park. Today it has become clear that the conservation of protected areas weighs most heavily on the local people who are no longer able to harvest plants and animals that formerly helped support village life. Working with these people to secure benefits for them must become an integral part of conservation projects (McNeely 1988).

Conflicting Goals: Government vs. Local Needs

The benefits rural people derive from nature are significant and varied. Using natural resources such as local wildlife and forest products to supplement their crops, rural people throughout the tropics have traditionally led a productive and diverse existence. Norman Myers, a well-known expert on conservation and development, compared the income available from wood and nonwood forest products and found that tropical forests can produce a self-renewing crop of wildlife with a potential value of slightly more than $200 per hectare, whereas the return from commercial logging is little more than $150 per hectare (Myers 1988). Fuel wood, timber, fish, game meat, animal skins, medicinal plants, honey, beeswax, fibers, gums, resins, rattan, fodder, mushrooms, fruits, and dyes are some of the many forest products that are used by people.

Indigenous Amazon Indian groups, for example, depend upon tropical forest trees for food, construction materials, medicinal plants, and trade goods (Prance et al. 1987). Firewood and mammal dung provide more than 90 percent of the total primary energy needs in Nepal, Tanzania, and Malawi and more than 80 percent in many other countries (Pearce 1987). In Botswana, more than 50 species of wild animals—from rodents to elephants—provide over 40 percent of the animal protein in the local people's diet, and one species in particular, a large squirrel-like rodent called the spring hare, provides more than three million kilograms (kg) of meat annually. In Zaire, game constitutes about 75 percent of the animal protein consumed (Sales 1981), and in Sarawak, Malaysia, wild pigs harvested by tribal hunters have a market value of approximately $100 million per year (Caldecott 1988).

Unfortunately, the benefits governments derive from protected areas often conflict with those of the local inhabitants, and establishing protected areas where human occupancy or use of resources is controlled by law can bring about real hardship. In Kenya, for example, tourism to the country's national parks is the leading foreign-exchange earner. Each lion in Amboseli National Park is worth an estimated $610,000, and net earnings from the park's tourism amount to a total of about $40 per hectare per year, some 50 times the net profit of the most optimistic projections for agricultural activities (Western 1984). Similarly, annual cash income from tourism to marine parks in the Caribbean includes such figures as $2 million for Caroni Swamp in Trinidad, $5 million for Bonaire Marine Park, $14 million for British Virgin Islands parks, and $50 million for Cayman Islands protected areas (Heyman 1988).

Water and soil protection provided by national parks also provide incentives for government protection. For example, the government of Venezuela recently tripled the size of the Canaima National Park to enhance its use for watershed protection and thus safeguard hydroelectric developments (Garcia 1984). Protected marine habitats can be particularly productive and beneficial. One study in India found that a partially protected mangrove forest produced 110 kg of prawns per hectare per year, while a similar unprotected mangrove forest produced only 20 kg (McNeely 1988). Similarly, in the Philippines, establishing coral reef protected areas increased the species diversity of fish from 25 to 40 percent in three sites, while increases in the numbers of all food fishes ranged from 42 percent to 293 percent (White and Law 1986).

These examples demonstrate clearly that conservation can return significant benefits to local people as well as to an entire nation. Research can also prove profitable in protected areas. For example, research projects in Costa Rica's Guanacaste National Park contribute approximately $200,000 per year to the local economy through purchase of supplies, employment of local assistants, and general contributions to the economy (Janzen 1988).

As ecotourism has grown, governments in tropical countries have found that establishing national parks and other protected areas can provide significant long-term benefits, especially through foreign-exchange earnings from tourists. Africa, tropical Asia, and tropical North and South America together now contain nearly 1,600 major conservation areas, a total area roughly three times the size of Texas. Establishing such areas is relatively easy. Convincing local people to support these government-sponsored conservation efforts when they stand to lose game or land potentially useful for agriculture remains a challenge. The greatest challenge is to find ways for local people to benefit from government conservation policies.

Khao Yai Revisited

After law enforcement attempts failed at Khao Yai, conservationists decided that the best approach was to give local villagers a stake in benefits from the park. In 1985, with help from the Population Community Development Association (a Thai organization experienced in rural development), conservationists devised a system that combined creative rural-development techniques with a conservation awareness program to encourage local cooperation in protecting park resources. The first stage of the project was a tourist trekking program designed to link economic benefits for the village to conservation of park resources. Villagers served as guides and porters for small groups of tourists who spent several days hiking through the park's mountains; wages were U.S.$5 per day, three times the average rate for typical village labor.

Through this initiative, villagers quickly realized that the tourists who came to see wildlife and forests would bring money to the village. However, additional incentives were needed to ensure that the trekking program was more profitable than illegal use of park resources. Thus, conservationists established a community-based, nongovernmental organization called the Environmental Protection Society to serve as a credit cooperative, an informal education center, and a collective business enterprise. Any villager who pledged to refrain from breaking park laws could become a member, and an annual election was held to form a 17-person committee to administer the society.

The group's principal goal was to provide viable alternatives to poaching by making start-up money available for income-generating projects, mainly in agriculture. A revolving fund was established as a credit cooperative with a $24,000 grant provided by a German rural development organization. Society members could borrow at 1 percent monthly interest (compared with 5 percent offered by

CHINA

Figure 6.1. Thailand's Khao Yai National Park (A) is located in a rural area where small populations of elephants, gibbons, tigers, gaur, and deer remain.

local middlemen) to buy seeds, fertilizer, and other essentials. Farmers would repay the loan after their produce was grown and sold, and all repayments would be returned to the revolving fund for the next round of lending. The society established a cooperative store, operated by members, to sell everyday goods at reasonable cost and to generate additional revenue for the organization. Members were offered shares in the store and received regular dividends. Community wood lots were established to satisfy economic and conservation goals, and a "food-for-work" program was created whereby villagers could perform community development work in exchange for rice.

The project's major conservation component, however, focused on awareness and extension activities for both adults and children. Khao Yai National Park staff began to offer periodic conservation awareness sessions to society members emphasizing the relationship between development and the care and maintenance of the natural environment. Society members and Khao Yai National Park staff also cooperated in a tree-planting program to demarcate the park boundary, especially in areas previously encroached upon by farmers, and members have helped park staff reforest parklands that were illegally cultivated. In addition, technical training has improved cultivation techniques, handicraft production, forest conservation, soil and wildlife protection, and basic business skills, and several villagers have been trained as village health volunteers to provide basic health and family-planning services.

The results of the Khao Yai project have been remarkable. Approximately 85 percent of all village households have participated in society functions. In 1986, the revolving fund loaned a total of $23,000 to members for crop production, cattle and chicken raising, maize cultivation for the school lunch program, and working capital for the cooperative store. All loans were repaid in full. Cooperation and communication among park officials and society members has virtually stopped encroachment along the park's boundaries, which are now recognized and respected by villagers. Poaching has been greatly reduced and, after more than a decade and a half, barking deer, elephants, and other native wildlife have returned to the edge of the village. Gibbons now whoop in the nearby forest as if to celebrate a promising new relationship between villagers and the forest ecosystem surrounding them.

Conclusion

The experiences at Khao Yai have taught several important lessons. First, not only *can* conservation pay, but it *must* pay if local people are to support conservation efforts. Second, successful approaches to conservation must be comprehensive and include a variety of development, training, and conservation activities for a broad sector of the local population. Third, local people must share responsibility for sound management of the natural resources that they depend upon. And, finally, governments need to ensure that the costs and benefits of conservation are equitably shared among local people and the nation at large.

Epilogue

Much has happened in the field of economics and protected areas since 1988. Several important books have been published on the subject (Dixon and Sherman 1990; Barbier et al. 1994). The Global Environment Facility was established in 1991 to channel funds to conservation, including some U.S.$315 million for conserving biological diversity (the majority of the funds went to protected areas). The IV World Congress on National Parks and Protected Areas was held in Caracas, Venezuela, in February 1992 (McNeely 1992). Relevant news presented at Caracas included:

- Expenditures in Nepal by tourists who come to visit protected areas are estimated at $9 million per year while the annual protected-area management budget is only about $3 million.
- In 1988 some 235 million people participated in international tourism to enjoy and appreciate nature, generating economic benefits amounting to as much as $233 billion.
- Trust funds to support protected areas have been established in Costa Rica, Bolivia, Ecuador, Jamaica, Mexico, Brazil, Argentina, Bhutan, Philippines, and Indonesia.
- In addition to numerous private lands managed for conservation purposes in the United States and the United Kingdom, 69 private protected areas have been identified in Latin America and 24 in Africa; many of these are adjacent to government-established protected areas but include tourism facilities that supplement the infrastructure of the established protected areas. Such private reserves generate up to 40 employee months per each 1,000 visitor nights, helping to generate considerable local employment and income.
- Efforts have continued to quantify economic benefits of protected areas in countries in which they are located. For example, the value of Galapagos National Park has been found to be U.S.$64 per hectare per year. And 8,728 hectares in the Sarawak Mangrove Forest Reserve in Malaysia provide annual benefits from marine fisheries worth $21.1 million, timber products worth $123,217, and a tourist industry worth $3.7 million (Munasinghe and McNeely 1994).
- Protected areas have a tremendously valuable economic characteristic: Because most of their benefits can be "consumed" by one person without affecting the ability of another to also benefit, these areas can be exploited by any number of people, both directly and indirectly. As part of the economic-development process, protected areas are essential to the security of nations.

References Cited

Barbier, E. B., J. C. Burgess, and K. Folke. 1994. *Paradise lost? The ecological economics of biodiversity*. London: Earthscan.

Caldecott, J. 1988. *Hunting and wildlife management in Sarawak*. Gland, Switzerland: International Union for the Conservation of Nature and Natural Resources (IUCN).

Dixon, J. A., and P. B. Sherman. 1990. *Economics of protected areas: A new look at benefits and costs*. Washington, D.C.: Island Press.

Garcia, J. R. 1984. Waterfalls, hydropower, and water for industry: Contributions from Canaima National Park. In *National parks, conservation, and development: The role of protected areas in sustaining society*, J. A. McNeely and K. R. Miller, eds. 588–591. Washington, D.C.: Smithsonian Institution Press.

Heyman, A. 1988. Self-financed resource management: A direct approach to maintaining marine biological diversity. Paper presented at the February 1988 Workshop on Economics, IUCN General Assembly, San Jose, Costa Rica.

Janzen, D. 1988. The use of economic incentives in Costa Rica's Guanacaste National Park. Paper presented at the February 1988 Workshop on Economics, IUCN General Assembly, San Jose, Costa Rica.

McNeely, J. A. 1988. *Economics and biological diversity: Developing and using economic incentives to conserve biological diversity*. Gland, Switzerland: International Union for the Conservation of Nature (IUCN).

McNeely, J. A., ed. 1992. Parks for life. *Proceedings of the IV World Congress on National Parks and Protected Areas*. Gland, Switzerland: International Union for the Conservation of Nature and Natural Resources.

Munasinghe, M., and J. A. McNeely. 1994. *Protected area economics and policy: Linking conservation and sustainable development*. Washington, D.C.: World Bank.

Myers, N. 1988. Tropical forests: Much more than stocks of wood. *Journal of Tropical Ecology* 4: 209–221.

Pearce, D. W. 1987. Economic values and the natural environment. Economics discussion paper, University College, London.

Prance, G. T., W. Balee, B. M. Boom, and R. L. Carneiro. 1987. Quantitative ethnobotany and the case for conservation in Amazonia. *Conservation Biology* 1: 296–310.

Praween P., T. Tavatchai, and R. J. Dobias. 1988. Using economic incentives to integrate park conservation and rural development in Thailand. Paper presented at the February 1988 Workshop on Economics, IUCN General Assembly, San Jose, Costa Rica.

Sales, J. B. 1981. *The importance and values of wild plants and animals in Africa*. Gland, Switzerland: International Union for the Conservation of Nature.

Western, D. 1984. Amboseli National Park: Human values and the conservation of a savanna ecosystem. In *National parks, conservation, and development: The role of protected areas in sustaining society*, J. A. McNeely and K. R. Miller, eds. 93–100. Washington, D.C.: Smithsonian Institution Press.

White, A. and D. Law. 1986. Evaluation of the marine conservation and development programme of Silliman University, Philippines. *MCDP Newsletter* 6: 1–15.

CHAPTER SEVEN

COMMUNITY CONSERVATION EDUCATION PROGRAM FOR THE GOLDEN LION TAMARIN IN BRAZIL: BUILDING SUPPORT FOR HABITAT CONSERVATION

Lou Ann Dietz

The golden lion tamarin (Figure 7.1) is a strikingly beautiful, squirrel-sized monkey native to lowland forests of the state of Rio de Janeiro in Brazil. Only 450 golden lion tamarins are confirmed to remain in the wild, all living in the Poço das Antas Federal Biological Reserve (Figure 7.2) or the municipalities surrounding it (Seal et al. 1990). Less than 2 percent of the original habitat of the tamarin remains today, limited to primary and secondary lowland forest patches. This forest is currently being cut and drained at an alarming rate to provide cattle pastures, rice fields, and commercial firewood, and the tamarin is considered one of the most endangered species of the rapidly disappearing Brazilian Atlantic Coastal Forest.

The Golden Lion Tamarin (GLT) Conservation Project is an international effort to conserve this ecosystem. Created in 1983, its goal is to save both the tamarin and the biological community it inhabits. The GLT project is coordinated by the National Zoological Park (Smithsonian Institution) in collaboration with the Brazilian Institute for the Environment and Renewable Natural Resources (IBAMA), the Rio de Janeiro Primatology Center (CPRJ-FEEMA), the Brazilian Foundation for Nature Conservation (FBCN), and 112 zoos worldwide that participate in a cooperative captive-breeding program. In addition, major support comes from the Smithsonian Institution's International Environmental Sciences Program, Friends of the National Zoo, World Wildlife Fund, Wildlife Preservation Trust International, the National Science Foundation, the Frankfurt Zoological Society, and the Canadian Embassy in Brazil. The National Zoological Park's biological and behavioral studies of captive golden lion tamarins since the early 1970s have made vital contributions to the program, providing information that has permitted the management of the captive population in a way that preserves genetic diversity (Kleiman and Jones 1977). The project is headquartered in the Poço das Antas Federal Biological Reserve, a 5,300-hectare (13,091 acre) area about 60 kilometers (km) north of the city of Rio de Janeiro. The reserve was established by the Brazilian federal government in 1974 specifically to protect tamarins.

Figure 7.1. Golden lion tamarin.

Drawing from its wide base of support and expertise, the project has adopted a multidisciplinary approach for comprehensive conservation efforts, including: studies of the ecology of golden lion tamarins in the wild; management and expansion of habitat in the Poço das Antas Biological Reserve and surrounding areas to increase carrying capacity for the species; developing techniques for reintroducing zoo-born golden lion tamarins into the wild and translocating wild tamarins into protected habitats; and developing a public-education program to build long-term support for the conservation of this species and its natural habitat.

Developing the Public-Education Program

From the program's outset, it was clear that without the support of people living in the region where golden lion tamarins still exist, all other efforts would have a limited impact on long-term conservation. The program's community education team was therefore established to work closely with other program participants as well as local people. Among the team's goals were to make the tamarin a symbol for forest conservation, to stimulate the development of desperately needed local conservation education activities throughout Brazil, and to create a model for solving conservation problems that require the support of local citizens. Success to date was made possible by a team of dedicated young Brazilians who began working in 1984 and continue to carry forward the public-education aspect of the GLT project today.

The following discussion uses a systems model to describe the program. This model has allowed project managers to focus efforts on priority problems, systematically develop appropriate solutions, and continually evaluate these solutions in order to increase their effectiveness.

Step 1: Defining Priority Problems

The first step toward generating community support was to define the most important conservation problems and determine whether they could be addressed with education campaigns. Ecological studies of the golden lion tamarin formed the basis for defining the major threats and priority actions, which included reducing deforestation in the lowland areas surrounding the Poço das Antas Reserve, ensuring permanent conservation of the remaining privately-owned lowland forests in the region, reducing fires in the forests and cleared areas of the region, reducing the illegal trade in golden lion tamarins, and reducing illegal hunting in the reserve.

Step 2: Identifying and Evaluating the Population Resources and Setting

After defining objectives, program participants conducted research to determine what resources and support would be available for its education component. To better understand the local population of the municipality of Silva Jardim surrounding the reserve, interviews were conducted in 1984 with the help of local volunteers. Questionnaires were distributed to a representative sample of 500 adult residents and 1,000 local school students. The results, along with informal discussions with community leaders, provided the basis for determining local knowledge, attitudes, and behaviors toward the forest, wildlife, and the reserve (Table 7.1). The information was also useful for determining the most appropriate communication methods for reaching the population and serving as a baseline study for later comparison.

While local people expressed no negative attitudes about the golden lion tamarin or the forest, the surveys did reveal that they knew little about forest conservation laws. Many residents were unaware that the reserve even existed. In response, the project set out to increase knowledge of the interrelationships among wildlife, habitat, and humans, as well as the importance of each ecological component of the forest to the proper functioning of the whole. Educational efforts stressed long-term and global consequences of local human actions on the environment and encouraged pride in local natural resources.

Initial interviews also indicated that the mass media were a potentially powerful means of reaching the general public: 80 percent of those interviewed watched television regularly, and 99 percent listened to the radio (Table 7.2). Considering the project's primary objectives, limited resources—and lack of local

Figure 7.2. The Golden Lion Tamarin Conservation Project focuses on protecting the Poço das Antas Biological Reserve, located in the state of Rio de Janeiro in Brazil.

phones, mail delivery, or passable roads—restricted contact largely to the populations of the three municipalities immediately surrounding the reserve (approximately 80,000 people). Media efforts were targeted toward the public at large as well as to two specific groups: citizens who might illegally purchase animals in the cities of Rio de Janeiro and São Paulo and government officials in Rio and Brasilia.

Step 3: Building a Positive Relationship

From the education program's outset in 1983, its leaders began building constructive relationships with local community leaders, including politicians, teachers, judges, police, businessmen, and clergy. Because human attitudes and behaviors change slowly, such community involvement in planning and implementing educational activities was crucial to ensure actions appropriate to local conditions as well as to stimulate long-term interest in the GLT project. Progam participants spent many weeks conducting informal conversations with these leaders to learn about the community, to explain project objectives and how they could help the community, and to ask for assistance. Soon, GLT project managers were being invited to participate in local community meetings, and they received many requests for information and presentations on conservation of the local environ-

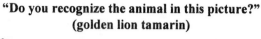

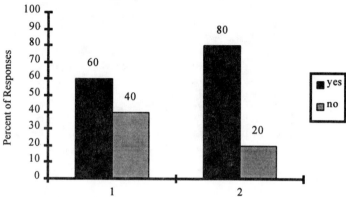

Table 7.1. Results of adult interviews on recognition of golden lion tamarins before (1) and after (2) implementation of the conservation education program.

ment. Community leaders also began to view the reserve and the GLT project as entities that could bring the community positive public attention. The relationships formed with influential local individuals proved to be helpful in many ways as the program developed. Nearly all of the 30-plus current education program participants are from the community. These people were motivated not only by jobs, but also by a desire to contribute to local conservation that was heightened by the status the project had attained in the community.

Step 4: Select and Test Methods

To select methods, the team identified those that both interested local leaders and seemed most likely to have the widest results for the least cost. Of central importance was a decision to make the golden lion tamarin a far-reaching symbol of forest conservation. The message was simple: To save the tamarins, we must save the forests, and by saving tamarins, we can begin to save all elements of the forest ecosystem. Not only is the golden lion tamarin an endemic forest-indicator species whose survival is linked directly to the survival of the rapidly disappearing Atlantic Coastal Forest, but it is also a strikingly beautiful and interesting animal. In contrast, an animal such as a snake generates little public sympathy, even though it may be just as important as any other forest component.

Created in response to requests by the community, educational materials were multipurpose, short, simple, and inexpensive. Because no information existed in Portuguese on local flora and fauna, the materials provided as much up-to-

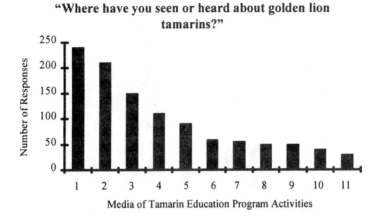

"Where have you seen or heard about golden lion tamarins?"

Media of Tamarin Education Program Activities

Table 7.2. Results of adult interviews reflecting where citizens got information about tamarins after implementation of the conservation education program. From left to right: television (1), photo (2), T-shirt (3), radio (4), print (5), film (6), school (7), parade (8), play (9), exhibit (10), trip (11).

date information as possible, including not-yet-published results of ecological studies under way in the reserve. The program produced printed materials for use in schools and for distribution to absentee landowners as well as audiovisual and live presentations for the community's adults, 41 percent of whom had no formal education. Prototypes of all these materials were tested and revised in both content and language—concepts perfectly understandable in Rio, for example, were not necessarily understandable in Silva Jardim, just 60 km away. To ensure communication of the intended message, even basic words such as *conservar* (to conserve) and *mata* (forest) had to be carefully explained, because they have local connotations sometimes nearly the opposite of the intended meanings. Other materials included press releases; video copies of news and other programs on conservation; public-service messages for radio and television; educational posters; pamphlets; school notebooks with an educational story on the cover; a slide collection for the reserve; slide-tape programs; information packages for landowners; a logo for the reserve that identifies all materials as relating to the conservation program; an electronic question/answer board; a traveling exhibit for local festivals; and T-shirts, stickers, and buttons recognizing contributions to conservation and local fundraising, which also serve as reminders of the larger conservation message. These materials have been used in a variety of combinations and activities with the expectation that some would be effective with different groups in the target population.

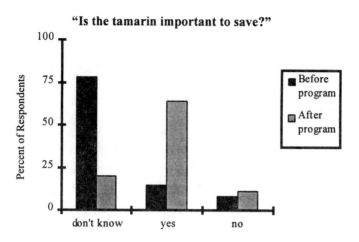

"Is the tamarin important to save?"

Table 7.3. Results of adult interviews regarding the belief that the tamarin is beneficial or important, both before and after implementation of the conservation education program.

Step 5: Implementing Activities

Educational activities initially targeted one of the three municipalities adjacent to the reserve. This experience provided momentum for establishing the program in the other two municipalities. Program leaders successfully worked with existing groups and institutions to achieve mutual objectives, and direct contact with the public has been accomplished with the help of interns, volunteers, and five young graduates of a local teacher-training high school. Activities are continually developed and modified as the need arises. They have included: classes for schools and farm workers; training classes for reserve guards, program personnel, and local teachers; lectures for local groups; educational field trips to the reserve for farmers, school groups, and families; use of habituated tamarins on a discovery trail to encourage detailed observation of the forest; press events; support for local conservation clubs; a children's play; parades organized by local teachers; and the planting of native trees for watershed protection. Education program participants have also made personal visits to landowners to encourage them to register their remaining forest patches as permanent reserves. If landowners do this, they receive captive-born or translocated wild-born tamarins for their land.

Step 6: Evaluation

A preliminary survey evaluation conducted two years after the program began indicated significant changes in the knowledge and attitudes of local adults as compared with the pre-program survey. There was a significant increase in the percentage of adult respondents able to correctly identify golden lion tamarins from a photo (Table 7.1), for example. More people also had knowledge of the animals' social organization and habitat. To measure changes in attitudes, respondents answered questions such as: "Is the golden lion tamarin important or beneficial?" Those who answered "no" had not changed their attitude significantly in two years, but there was a significant decrease in the percentage who responded "don't know" as well as an increase in those who responded "yes" (Table 7.3). Many who responded "yes" in the post-interviews still gave reasons related to beauty or pleasure in seeing the animal, but others gave reasons such as "the tamarin is part of nature" or "it has a right to live," answers not given at all in the pre-interviews. To learn which methods had reached the most adults, those who correctly identified the tamarin were asked where they had seen or heard of the monkey, whether it was related to the GLT project or not. The most often mentioned sources were television, photos, or posters, as well as T-shirts, stickers, and buttons. Respondents cited television almost as often as all nonproject activities combined (Table 7.2).

Since the education program began, local people have voluntarily turned over to the reserve more than 20 illegally-held golden lion tamarins and 25 maned sloths (another endangered species endemic to the region). Some landowners have registered their forests as permanent reserves, and many have requested tamarins for their land (nine landowners have actually received tamarins, and 15 others are on a waiting list). The program receives many requests for advice, materials, internships, and information. In addition, many conservation activities have been initiated by the citizens and communities themselves—not only in the primary target region immediately outside the reserve, but even in Rio de Janeiro, where the project has had no contact with the public except through exhibits and the mass media. The Brazilian Forest Service, which previously barred visitors to the reserve, has constructed the first building dedicated to community and visitor education in any Brazilian national biological reserve. Local Brazilian staff now run the conservation education program completely, and it is hoped that they will eventually be hired by the Forest Service to continue this education effort as regular employees.

Step 7: Recycling

Continual evaluations have already helped improve methods as the program has been developed. The results of the first formal evaluation of the program as a whole have enabled managers to determine the cost-effectiveness of individual activities as well as decide which conservation education efforts should continue in the region over the long term. This information also allows the education team to provide recommendations for those developing public conservation education programs in other areas of Brazil.

Conclusion

Although the Golden Lion Tamarin Community Conservation Education Program has demonstrated considerable success since it began in 1983, its work has only just begun. The local public is now at a critical point of awareness about the problems of disappearing forest, and the program team has accepted the responsibility of ensuring that tamarins and their forest will have a future. Widespread changes in human behavior require a continued effort over the long term, however, and the action of many more people is needed to guarantee the conservation of enough forest for the golden lion tamarin to survive.

Epilogue

To guarantee the long-term viability of the population of golden lion tamarins in the wild, we know that we need to have 2,000 golden lion tamarins in 23,000 hectares of protected forest by the year 2000. Reintroduction efforts have resulted in a 30 percent increase in the wild population. In 1995, for the first time since the project began, there were more golden lion tamarins in the wild than in captivity. Captives are now bred in 30 institutions worldwide, including Brazilian zoos.

The Golden Lion Tamarin Conservation Project marked its 13th year in 1996. During these years, ecological studies providing critical knowledge of the tamarins and their habitat were completed. These results mean that priority actions and target dates required to achieve long-term conservation of a viable *in situ* population of golden lion tamarins are much more precise than they used to be (Golden Lion Tamarin Conservation Program, 1991).

In coordination with the other GLT project components, the education program continues to build local support for forest conservation in the region. This effort involves a constant process of prioritizing target audiences and specific behavior changes needed, evaluating the effectiveness of actions to achieve these changes, and adjusting strategies accordingly.

Recently the program has given the highest priority to encouraging the owners of remaining forest to establish private reserves on all tracts larger than 50 hectares within the habitat range of the golden lion tamarins. To ensure the survival of the golden lion tamarin for the next 200 years, the protection of the remaining forest and regeneration of additional forest must be achieved by the year 2025. This short time frame has meant the reduction of activities with local children and the increase of education work with adults. (For project activities since

1990, see Golden Lion Tamarin Conservation Program 1991; Ballou 1993; and Dietz and Nagagata 1995.) One of the major developments was the establishment of the Golden Lion Tamarin Association in 1991, with the goal of assuring sustainability of local action until the survival of golden lion tamarins is assured. A large portion of the association members are local landowners and other community members.

Acknowledgments

I would like to acknowledge the collaboration of the Golden Lion Tamarin Conservation Education Program team: Elizabeth Yoshimi Nagagata, Denise Rambaldi, Lenimar Christina dos Santos Alcântara, Norma Silva Araujo, Rita Cássia S. Gonçalves, Percília Maria F. Machado, and Maria Sônia de Oliveira. Without the dedication and talents of these young Brazilians, none of what has been described above would have been possible. The continued efforts of this program are now in their hands.

References Cited

Ballou, J. D. 1993. *1992 International golden lion tamarin studbook.* Washington, DC: National Zoological Park.

Dietz, L. A. and E. Y. Nagagata. 1995. Golden lion tamarin conservation program: A community education effort for forest conservation. In *Conserving wildlife: International education/communication approaches*, S.K. Jacobson, ed. 95–124. New York: Columbia University Press.

Golden Lion Tamarin Conservation Program. 1991. Mission statement. Washington, D.C.: Smithsonian Institution.

Kleiman, D. G., and M. Jones. 1977. The current status of *Leontopithecus rosalia* with comments on breeding success at the National Zoological Park. In *The biology and conservation of the callitrichidae*, D. G. Kleiman, ed. Washington, D.C.: Smithsonian Institution Press.

Seal, U. S., J. D. Ballou, and C. V. Padua. 1990. *Leontopithecus* population viability analysis workshop report. Captive Breeding Specialist Group, Species Survival Commission. International Union for Conservation of Nature and Natural Resources (IUCN).

CHAPTER EIGHT

SELF-MANAGEMENT AND GOVERNMENT MANAGEMENT OF
WILDLIFE: PROSPECTS FOR COORDINATION IN JAMES BAY AND
CANADA

Harvey A. Feit

One of the most important debates in conservation today centers on whether effective linkages can be developed between indigenous systems of wildlife management and those instituted by government authorities. As this chapter explains, such linkages must deal with the fact that both parties claim and exercise relative autonomy yet are also, in many respects, mutually dependent on each other. However simple this may sound, conservationists trying to build connections between the two sides must confront complex issues, ranging from recognizing the knowledge and practices of other cultures to assertions of aboriginal rights to manage wildlife. Many of these issues have come to light over the past few decades in northern Quebec in the relationship between the James Bay Cree and the government of Canada.

Cultural Knowledge and Social Practices

The James Bay Cree are a group of about 10,000 subarctic Native Americans in northern Quebec who hunt in an area of approximately 150,000 square miles east and south of James Bay (Figure 8.1). Their use and management of wildlife provides a valuable example of the importance of culturally and socially specific systems in organizing hunting practices for the prudent use of resources (Berkes 1977, 1982; Feit 1978, 1986a; Scott 1987).

To the Cree people, knowledge is based on a world view in which all phenomena involving action can be associated with person-beings or power-beings (Hallowell 1955, 1976; Black 1967; Feit 1978). In other words, events and their causes are not attributed to natural or mechanical phenomena, but rather to the personal will of winds, weather systems, tools, animals, and other phenomena considered to be culturally active beings. Animals are thought to be capable of interpreting and understanding the actions of humans, and animal actions are interpreted as the result of willful choices. For example, Cree hunters only catch an

Figure 8.1. The James Bay Cree, approximately 10,000 in number, inhabit a 150,000-square-mile area in northern Quebec, east and south of James Bay. Shown are the Cree communities in that area.

animal when the animal gives itself to them or is given to them by the Supreme Being and the spirits. Similarly, they are given animals because they respectfully ask for what they need to survive, and their requests are heard. The Cree treat animals with respect in the way they hunt, butcher, consume, and use the carcasses, for they believe that the animals they hunt (whose souls can survive and be reborn) both expect and appreciate it. When animals are reborn, respectful and grateful humans can continue to find them a source of sustenance. The balance is reciprocal: When hunters act properly, animals continue to be born in healthy numbers, enabling humans to lead healthy lives (Feit 1986a). To prevent overhunting, the Cree believe they receive guidelines or signs from animals and spirits to help them determine how much they are being given. Understanding these communications from the spirits requires complex observations and interpretations of weather, and plant and animal populations.

The Cree's cultural system of understanding nature differs fundamentally from that of Western science. While Western science links animals, vegetation, and inorganic habitats in an "ecosystem model," the Cree incorporate all potentially active spirits and entities that they experience into a unified "social cosmos," where standard indicators such as cohort sizes, aggregation sizes, age and sex ratios, and frequency of encounters are considered not mere biological phenomena but actual messages from the animals and spirit masters.

Also in contrast to many Western views, the Cree value land not as a commodity to be individually owned, but as a common resource whose management and conservation is in the hands of designated stewards. Each one inherits stewardship of a more or less defined tract or hunting territory from a parent or elder kinsman and allocates access to other hunters through a system of indigenous community legal rights and privileges (Feit 1991; Scott 1991). Only one in five Cree adult males is a steward—usually a hunter who has used an area for many years (Figure 8.2). Through this system of resource management, the steward becomes the central repository of knowledge about a specific tract of land and its wildlife through his own, first-hand experience as well as that of the hunters he leads. In using this knowledge to effectively manage game populations and help others hunt and survive, he also exemplifies highly valued Cree virtues, as his wisdom is said to express insights communicated to him from powerful spiritual beings who sanction his authority and power.

The effectiveness of traditional Cree practices has been well documented in a detailed study of the Waswanipi community of James Bay Cree. During the study periods in 1968–69 and 1969–70, total harvests of both moose and beaver—the main subsistence game—were well within estimated sustainable yields, a remarkable fact given that the community had to purchase approximately half of its food to feed a growing population (Feit 1987a). Furthermore, repeated aerial surveys conducted by the Quebec and Canadian Wildlife Services during the 1960s and early 1970s showed that moose and beaver populations remained stable, indicating that the Cree territorial system of management was clearly effective in maintaining animal populations at sustainable levels over the long term (Audet 1976; Feit 1986b, 1987b).

Cree and Governmental Management: Historical Linkages

The Cree system of wildlife management has been linked to systems established by the governments of Quebec and Canada for more than 50 years. However, a formal and mutually agreed upon recognition of both systems and the establishment of specific mechanisms of coordination or co-management were not negotiated until 1975. This formal agreement was part of a process leading to the first modern treaty in Canada, the James Bay and Northern Quebec Agreement (JBNQA).

Figure 8.2. A Cree hunter on the lookout for geese duiring the autumn near Waswanipi.

The initial establishment of government policy in the northern Quebec region took place in the 1920s and 1930s, when both the federal and provincial governments declared much of the area an exclusive trapping reserve for indigenous inhabitants. This policy helped to re-establish the renewable resource base by excluding competing, non-native trappers and regenerating the indigenous economy after a period of natural game declines and destructive, unregulated competition from non-native commercial trappers. Unlike other regions where commercial-style traplines were imposed, provincial and national governments responded in a more culturally informed and appropriate way, basing the new program on existing hunting territory structures of the Indian peoples. The initiative was welcomed both by the governments involved and the indigenous peoples.

Yet its immediate beneficial consequences obscured some fundamental differences in how the governments and indigenous peoples viewed the policy. From the point of view of the provincial and federal governments, it was a new, legally formalized wildlife management system that was based upon but replaced an outdated indigenous system. The governments assumed legal authority for land and wildlife resources, an authority they believed was legitimized by the Western legal system. Indigenous peoples, on the other hand, perceived the governments as well-intended, well-informed, metaphoric kinsmen, who had acted with appropriate concern for a poorer relative by restraining the cupidity of non-native trappers (Feit 1986a, 1982). They recognized that their own system of hunting needed links to Canadian governmental authority that could regulate non-natives who were beyond the influence of the indigenous management system. They also believed that government intervention had strengthened their own management practices and that they were continuing to manage wildlife based on their own system. The Cree system derived its legitimacy from spiritual ties to powerful beings and from Cree customary law, however, and not from any delegation of authority or recognition by distant governments.

When government-authorized, nonrenewable resource development accelerated in the 1960s, these conflicting perceptions became increasingly evident. Along with opening the region for development, wildlife managers began restricting Cree hunters in order to enhance opportunities for growing numbers of nonnative sportsmen. The conflict escalated in 1971 with the unilaterally initiated James Bay Hydroelectric Project, viewed by the Cree as part of a process of dispossession. The project provoked court actions against the government as the Cree demanded their aboriginal rights to the land and its resources and warned of the irremediable damages the project would cause to their culture and way of life.

Initial court rulings supported these aboriginal claims and set the stage for two years of intensive negotiations among the Cree, the Inuit of northern Quebec, and the provincial and federal governments. The final result was the James Bay and Northern Quebec Agreement of 1975 which, among other things, established agreements for management of wildlife, lands, and hunting. Over most of the territory, the responsibility for regulating fell to the government. The indigenous management system of the Cree was acknowledged as the primary means for Cree to regulate themselves. When joint action was needed, it was thought that non-native and indigenous peoples would voluntarily comply with jointly agreed upon regulations. The agreement also instituted a continuing consultative process, created to foster effective co-management and cooperation between the indigenous peoples and the government and establish linkages between the two systems of management. In addition, certain species and areas were designated exclusively for indigenous use, an environmental and social impact assessment procedure was initiated, and a unique guaranteed annual income program was established for Cree who pursued hunting as a way of life (Scott 1984; Feit 1988). The various interests and trade-offs that underlay the negotiating process behind the agreement are identified elsewhere (Feit 1980, 1989).

Assessing Coordinated Management in Northern Quebec

In signing the agreement, the Cree sought to preserve their distinctive culture and economy through greater cooperation and mutual respect. The government sought recognition of its authority and more effective local implementation of policies through coordinated management. While events since the agreement have promoted some of these desired outcomes, both indigenous peoples and government authorities have attained only a portion of their goals (Feit 1988). Cree

A   B

Figure 8.3. Geese (A) and moose (B) are two principal game animals hunted by the James Bay Cree.

hunters have benefited by the continuation of their hunting way of life and by the institution of the guaranteed annual income program. After a decade of decline prior to the agreement, the number of Cree whose primary productive activity is hunting initially increased by 43 percent and then stabilized. No general or widespread overutilization of game resources by the Cree has been noted, and the system of management through hunting territories has generally functioned properly. The agreement has enhanced traditional social norms, but important changes have also resulted from more formalized, community-level decision-making processes.

Uncertainty about the impact of future development continues, however. One reason is that the agreement's provisions, including the requirement for social and environmental impact assessment, have not substantially modified the kinds of possible large-scale resource development—forestry and hydroelectric projects—envisioned in the region. Long delays have weakened the agreement's coordinated management provisions, which have slowed its legal and organizational implementation. Most new wildlife management research conducted during the first years after the agreement's signing was carried out by indigenous peoples' organizations, not by the governments. Despite having claimed significant increases in their obligations for policing and research activities, government authorities have, in fact, committed very few additional resources to fulfilling their new responsibilities. Government policy making for managing the region's wildlife continues to be characterized by a failure to balance different interests as policies reflect a predominance of political interests over conservation goals. Resistance to changes in government management procedures has undermined efforts to involve indigenous peoples effectively in both the policy-making process and the economic development of the region's renewable resources. Furthermore, provisions that would have limited government policy initiatives to promote non-indigenous commercial uses of wildlife, or that would have increased indigenous participation in these uses, have been ignored or subverted. On several occasions, indigenous organizations have had to seek legal recourse through the courts to remedy violations of the agreement.

So far, the Cree system of self-management has, to the extent possible, ensured conservation of game resources. However, Cree aspirations and hopes are constantly threatened by increasing sport hunting and political and economic developments. The coordinated pursuit of conservation and development has yet to be established, and many questions remain regarding the kind of coordinated wildlife management that may be practical between culturally distinct peoples.

Indigenous Peoples and Wildlife Conservation in the Canadian North

North Americans of European descent have long viewed indigenous peoples' hunting, fishing, and trapping ways of life as anachronistic behaviors, doomed in time to give way to more intensive, efficient, and reliable modes of living. This dim assessment has helped encourage policies that not only have removed land and resources from indigenous control, but also have sought a rapid assimilation of indigenous peoples into Canadian society. While such policies have been promoted by rigorous national legislation and administration, they have fundamentally failed to integrate the indigenous population. Over the last two decades, recognition of this failure has been accompanied by a resurgence in indigenous political mobilization. Historical, cultural, economic, legal, and political factors have all focused attention on the control and use of both land and wildlife as central issues. For northern Canadian indigenous hunters, land and wildlife are the vital links to culture, economy, and politics. They feel a close connection between their communities' ability to maintain cultural and economic autonomy and their right to use and control their land and wildlife.

Indigenous peoples and social scientists agree that several factors are essential to effective land and wildlife use policy in northern Canada: reaffirmation of spiritual and religious beliefs through practices and experiences tied to land-based living; continual re-creation of the social fabric of kin and community through the allocation of hunting rights, sharing of work, and distribution of harvests; recognition of the practical value of an economy based on wildlife resources for local self-sufficiency and reassurance that there are means to meet economic goals that opportunities in the cash sector alone cannot meet; and the essential contribution of wild foods to nutrition and health in isolated northern populations (Richardson 1976, 1989; Freeman 1979, 1985; Tanner 1979; Worl 1980; Brody 1981; Scott 1982; Langdon 1986; Hawkes 1991; Cooper 1991). Legal assertion of aboriginal rights has also reinforced awareness of the importance of land and wildlife, as aboriginal legal claims are enhanced by demonstrations of continued use and occupancy of a territory and its resources (Hutchins 1988).

These developments have introduced a succession of topics into Canadian public discussions since the 1970s, including the legal and moral status of aboriginal rights, the goals of northern economic development, the interplay of national and regional interests in governmental policy making, the compatibility of indigenous self-governance with legitimacy of the Canadian state, the means of remedying economic and social inequality between indigenous and national populations, and the viability of indigenous resource use and management and its consequences for government wildlife management policies. Land and wildlife use and management have now become central political issues in discussions of northern development and aboriginal rights in Canada. Wildlife biologists and managers, conservationists, indigenous peoples, politicians, and social scientists have all found that conventional wildlife and conservation science does not provide adequate models or policies for handling the complexity of this problem (Berkes 1981, 1984; Freeman 1985; Usher 1986).

Conflicting Legal Cultures and Legal Systems

In North America, wildlife management, conservation, and land use planning systems have developed largely within the context of the British legal tradition, the administrative structure of the nation state, and the ideological authority of Western science. Indigenous peoples' assertion of aboriginal rights to use land and wildlife in Canada has recently brought attention to several fundamental differences between their own management practices and those of the government.

For example, although most indigenous peoples accept citizenship and participation in the political system of the nation, they do not necessarily accept the present distribution of rights established by the existing legislation. With respect to wildlife, indigenous cultural knowledge and practices are incompatible with assertions by government officials that they must authorize all allocations for wildlife use. Indigenous populations typically do not accept that their rights to wildlife are either conceded or delegated to them by legislation, departmental regulations, or policies. Canadian courts have generally ruled that whatever rights indigenous peoples have to wildlife, they are subservient to the rights government grants to land-based resource users such as mining or logging interests (Usher 1984; Hutchins 1988). These rulings conflict with aboriginal hunters' own systems of rights and authority over land and wildlife use and present problems even when indigenous peoples seek regionally appropriate forms of economic development (Usher 1981; Hutchins 1988).

Much of the new literature exploring the need to consider indigenous cultures in wildlife and conservation planning proceeds either from the idea that it is practically desirable and mutually beneficial to do so or from equally important moral grounds for doing so (see articles in Hanks 1984; McNeely and Pitt 1985;

and the Alberta Society of Professional Biologists 1986). Linking the legal systems of indigenous peoples and government for allocating rights to use and manage natural resources has little precedent within wildlife sciences, conservation traditions, or the international legal system. Moreover, the obligations under indigenous legal systems and international law for such linkages have yet to be systematically considered.

Conflicting Cultural Values and Subsistence Management Practices

Further problems in coordinated management stem from the fact that conservation strategies are specific to the legal, bureaucratic, and scientific contexts in which they are developed; thus, they are specific to the types of management problems that authorities try to resolve. Unlike governments, which may be more concerned with conservation of natural resources in the context of their use by commercial or recreational users, indigenous peoples depend on natural resources for significant portions of their subsistence needs as well as for marketable products (see Marks 1976, 1984). Not only is subsistence hunting regulated by culturally defined needs (as opposed to maximum harvest levels), it is organized around a domestic economy as opposed to a market economy. Because they are based on the needs of local society, production levels are not determined by a theoretically limitless market demand. Most hunting is conducted to meet culturally defined food and cash needs, and, when these needs are met, harvesting ceases (Scott 1982, 1984).

Such fundamental cultural differences in wildlife management surface in the frequent perception by indigenous hunters that governments regulate natural resources inappropriately. Restrictions on hunting seasons and bag limits, for example, decrease the efficiency of the harvester. While indigenous hunters may recognize that such limits work well for a sport hunter or fisherman, they do not make sense for the subsistence hunter. A typical response to what are perceived as inappropriate regulations is to surreptitiously harvest game or fail to report harvests fully.

Similarly, government wildlife officials often fail to consider the consequences of their regulations on a subsistence economy. Restricting access to an early spring fish run, for instance, may reduce a community's food supply at a time when food is most limited and may, in certain cases, cause an unacceptable seasonal deterioration in the nutritional intake of community members. Similarly, wildlife conservation officers may not support community restrictions on harvesting a resource, such as not taking trophy animals that are herd leaders or not killing geese in large aggregations. Government managers may consider such restrictions too limiting on sport hunters' time or trophy takes. They may reject the restrictions even though indigenous hunters say, on the basis of their experience, that removing lead animals can increase the chances of changing migratory patterns or that hunting geese in the main flock will make many birds shyer and harder to hunt in the future.

Conclusions: Joint Management or Dual Management?

The differences between subsistence hunters' and government officials' wildlife management practices have not yet been resolved. Neither side has an adequate understanding of the other's positions, and fundamentally different interests block easy resolution. Indeed, the different roots of the two systems of knowledge and action suggest that while each might gain from understanding how the other works, the systems cannot be readily integrated or combined. Current problems stem from the fact that wildlife managers have not fully considered assertions by indigenous peoples that they currently have, or could re-establish, systems of effective management and conservation of wildlife and land.

Unfortunately, these issues are being discussed and policy is being debated on the basis of wholly inadequate data, and people are taking positions based on casual experiences without insisting that the issues be systematically investigated. Anecdotal evidence of indigenous peoples' wildlife misuse or wise conservation tells us very little about overall patterns or causes of events. This unsystematic approach to assessing indigenous wildlife management knowledge and practices also fails to evaluate the potential means of coordinating indigenous self-management with government-mandated systems. As a result, these systems are uncoordinated and often work at cross purposes, a situation that is detrimental to both parties.

Furthermore, while international conservation agencies and governments often cite the goal of including local participation in government management, such joint management is often insufficient in practice. In parts of Canada, for example, the long process of parallel local and government wildlife management has already generated direct legal and political conflicts (Usher 1986; Osherenko 1988; Pinkerton 1989). The James Bay and Northern Quebec experience also indicates that, even when such joint participation is established, it may be difficult to implement effectively. The difficulties occur both at the point of decentralizing bureaucratic decision making and in the continued influence of wider political and economic interests in wildlife management decisions. For example, governmental responsiveness to the needs of wildlife and the concerns of indigenous peoples can be severely restricted by its interests in resource development and by its political sensitivity to the interests of commercial and recreational users (see also Power 1979; Berkes 1989).

Proposals that local and government management systems should develop extensive co-management systems seem to be limited by the same constraints. Such proposals may not be easily implemented or even widely supported, given the fundamentally different values and interests of the two systems. Another alternative not yet sufficiently explored may be to seek dual management, which would feature more enhanced, local self-management and more responsive government management, with the two linked only in specific decision environments. It is striking that the James Bay and Northern Quebec Agreement has enhanced Cree self-management of land and wildlife. Still, it has not resolved all of the problems the Cree encounter when they must work with government-mandated management systems, which have been inconsistent and unresponsive to legal obligations under the agreement to establish effective co-management. These lessons indicate that the Cree are better off with their own self-management and with limited coordination with the government.

Given these conflicts, it is clear that what is needed in conservation management for situations involving culturally distinct societies is a model of parallel self- and government-mandated wildlife management. Such a model would contain links not only in specific arenas, but would also recognize the existence, authority, and mandates of both systems. In fact, the idea of continuing, developing, and extending self-management is now being actively pursued by several indigenous groups across Canada. At present, the continued and enhanced existence of self-management systems provides the best protection available to fulfill diverse cultural aspirations and the long-term pursuit of better coordination between indigenous and government-mandated management systems.

Epilogue

Recent efforts to coordinate wildlife management in the James Bay region have shown how political and economic constraints in government management—hand in hand with disrespect for local Indian management systems—can lead to a breakdown of government responsibility with regard to one species: in this case, coordinated management of the region's moose population has failed.

From at least 1974 the Cree have expressed to the Quebec government their concerns about the condition of the region's moose population. However, for a variety of reasons, the government refused to respond to these early warnings and instead pursued a policy of increasing access to the region by moose sport hunters. Sport hunting was expanded despite the fact that public forests of the southern portions of this region were being cut with increasing intensity by international corporations granted permits by Quebec. Although the Cree were able to sustain relatively stable moose harvests throughout the period following the mid-1970s, when they sought government cooperation for conservation measures, surveys conducted in the early 1990s have revealed alarming declines in the moose population (Lajoie 1994).

Initial proposals made by the Quebec government in response to these declines have been seriously inadequate given what is known about the demographics of the moose population (Messier 1993; Lajoie 1994). Furthermore, government proposals ignored provisions of the 1975 treaty with the Cree, including one that requires sport hunting to be reduced to minimize harm to Cree subsistence hunters. An adequate and legal response has not been formulated at this time, and the long-term future of the moose population is unclear.

This situation has serious consequences for a growing number of experiments elsewhere attempting to coordinate local and state wildlife management. When the Cree and the governments of Quebec and Canada were negotiating their respective responsibilities, it was the position of government conservation officers that they should have full and final responsibility, maintaining that only the government department responsible for wildlife management could act consistently in the interests of wildlife. In response, some Cree negotiators felt that joint management would be an acceptable compromise given their common interest in game conservation. On the basis of the latter assumption, they sought and agreed to a system of limited co-management.

The assumption that government wildlife agencies are consistently committed to conserving game has been put into question by these recent developments in Canada. It is already well recognized that government agencies generally give wildlife conservation a lower priority than other land and resource uses, such as forestry and hydroelectric development. The developments in James Bay show that even the department responsible for wildlife conservation may put the interests of sport hunters and its bureaucracy ahead of wildlife. When conservation ceases to be the priority of the government agencies charged with wildlife management, the basis of all cooperation threatens to dissolve. It is a tragic lesson, but hopefully not a permanent condition.

Acknowledgments

This chapter draws on research funded by the Social Sciences and Humanities Research Council of Canada (Grants 410-81-0241, 410-84-0547, 410-87-0715, 410-90-0802, and 410-93-0505) and by the Arts Research Board of McMaster University. I wish to thank both institutions. In preparing this chapter, I have drawn extensively on discussions held over the course of several years with Cree administrators and colleagues involved in implementing and reviewing the James Bay and Northern Quebec Agreement. At the cost of omitting many who helped, I would like to specially thank Philip Awashish, Thomas Berger, Fikret Berkes, Taylor Brelsford, Lorraine Brooke, Brian Craik, Thomas Coon, Rick Cuciurean, Billy Diamond, Peter Hutchins, William Kemp, Abel Kitchen, Steve Langdon, Ignatius LaRusic, James O'Reilly, Alan Penn, Richard Preston, Richard

Salisbury, Colin Scott, Adrian Tanner, Peter Usher, Martin Weinstein, and Paul Wilkinson. An earlier version of this chapter was given at the Society for Applied Anthropology meetings in Santa Fe, New Mexico, in April, 1989.

References Cited

Alberta Society of Professional Biologists. 1986. *Native people and renewable resource management: The 1986 Symposium of the Alberta Society of Professional Biologists.* Edmonton, Alberta: Alberta Society of Professional Biologists.

Audet, R. 1976. Distribution de l'original dans la region de la Baie James, de la riviere Eastmain a l'Harricana. Quebec: Quebec Ministere du Tourisme, de la Chasse et de la Peche.

Berkes, F. 1977. Fishery resource use in a subarctic Indian community. *Human Ecology* 5: 289–307.

Berkes, F. 1981. The role of self-regulation in living resources management in the North. In *Renewable resources and the economy of the north*, M. M. R. Freeman, ed. 166–178. Ottawa: Association of Canadian Universities for Northern Studies and Man and Biosphere Program.

Berkes, F. 1982. Waterfowl management and northern native peoples with reference to Cree hunters of James Bay. *Musk Ox* 30: 23–35.

Berkes, F. 1984. Alternative styles in living resources management: The case of James Bay, Quebec. *Environments* 16: 114–123.

Berkes, F. 1989. Co-management and the James Bay Agreement. In *Co-operative management of local fisheries*, E. Pinkerton, ed. 189–208. Vancouver: University of British Columbia Press.

Black, M. B. 1967. An ethnoscience investigation of Ojibwa ontology and world view. Ph.D. dissertation. Stanford, Calif.: Stanford University.

Brody, H. 1981. *Maps and dreams: Indians and the British Columbia frontier.* Toronto: Douglas and McIntyre.

Cooper, G. 1991. Cree stories. *Northeast Indian Quarterly* 8: 30–33.

Cree Trappers Association. 1989. *Cree trappers speak.* Chisasibi: James Bay Cree Cultural Association.

Feit, H. A. 1978. Waswanipi realities and adaptations: Resource management and cognitive structure. Ph.D. dissertation. Montreal: McGill University.

Feit, H. A. 1980. Negotiating recognition of aboriginal rights: History, strategies, and reactions to the James Bay and Northern Quebec Agreement. *Canadian Journal of Anthropology* 1: 159–172.

Feit, H. A. 1982. The future of hunters within nation states: Anthropology and the James Bay Cree. In *Politics and history in band societies,* E. Leacock and R. B. Lee, eds. 373–417. Cambridge: Cambridge University Press.

Feit, H. A. 1986a. Hunting and the quest for power: The James Bay Cree and Whitemen in the twentieth century. In *Native peoples: The Canadian experience,* R. B. Morrison and C. R. Wilson, eds. 171–207. Toronto: McClelland and Stewart.

Feit, H. A. 1986b. James Bay Cree Indian management and moral considerations of fur bearers. In *Native people and renewable resource management: The 1986 Symposium of the Alberta Society of Professional Biologists.* 49–65. Edmonton: Alberta Society of Professional Biologists.

Feit, H. A. 1987a. Waswanipi Cree management of land and wildlife: Cree cultural ecology revisited. In *Native Peoples: Native Lands,* B. Cox, ed. 75–91. Ottawa: Carleton University Press.

Feit, H. A. 1987b. North American native hunting and management of moose populations. *Swedish Wildlife Research* 1: 25–42.

Feit, H. A. 1988. The power and the responsibility: Implementation of the wildlife and hunting provisions of the James Bay and Northern Quebec Agreement. In *James Bay and Northern Quebec Agreement: Ten years after,* S. Vincent and G. Bowers, eds. 74–88. Montreal: Recherches Amerindiennes au Quebec.

Feit, H. A. 1989. James Cree self-governance and management of land and wildlife. In *We are here: Politics of aboriginal land tenure,* E. N. Wilmsen, ed. 68–98. Berkeley: University of California Press.

Feit, H. A. 1991. Gifts of the land: Hunting territories, guaranteed incomes and the construction of social relations in James Bay Cree society. In *Cash, commoditisation and changing foragers*, N. Peterson and T. Matsuyama, eds. 223–268. Senri Ethnological Studies, Osaka: National Museum of Ethnology.

Freeman, M. M. R. 1979. Traditional land users as a legitimate source of environmental expertise. In *The Canadian National Parks Today and Tomorrow Conference II: Ten years later, Vol. I*, G. Nelson, R. D. Needham, S. H. Nelson, and R. C. Scace, eds. 345–369. Waterloo, Ontario: Waterloo University Studies in Land Use, History and Landscape Change.

Freeman, M. M. R. 1985. Appeal to tradition: Different perspectives on arctic wildlife management. In *Native power: The quest for autonomy and nationhood of indigenous peoples*, J. Brosted, J. Dahl, A. Gray, H. C. Gullov, G. Henricksen, J. B. Jorgensen, and I. Kleivan, eds. 265–281. Bergen, Norway: Universitetsforlaget.

Hallowell, A. I. 1955. *Culture and experience*. Philadelphia: University of Pennsylvania Press.

Hallowell, A. I. 1976. *Contributions to anthropology: Selected papers of A. Irving Hallowell*. Chicago: University of Chicago Press.

Hanks, J. 1984. Traditional life-styles, conservation and rural development. Commission on Ecology. Paper No. 7. Gland, Switzerland: International Union for the Conservation of Nature.

Hawkes, S. 1991. Unheard voices: James Bay II and the women of Kuujjvarapik. *Northern Perspectives* 19: 9–11.

Hutchins, P. W. 1988. The law applying to trapping of furbearing animals by aboriginal peoples: A case of double jeopardy. In *Wild furbearer management and conservation in North America*, M. Novak and J. A. Baker, eds. 31–38. Toronto: Ontario Ministry of Natural Resources, Wildlife Branch.

Lajoie, Ginette. 1994. Personal communication, Grand Council of the Crees (of Quebec), Montreal.

Langdon, S. J. 1986. Contradictions in Alaskan native economy and society. In *Contemporary Alaskan native economies*, S.J. Landgon, ed. 29–46. Lanham, Md.: University Press of America.

Marks, S. 1976. *Large mammals and a brave people: Subsistence hunters in Zambia*. Seattle: University of Washington Press.

Marks, S. 1984. *The imperial lion: Human dimensions of wildlife management in Central Africa*. Boulder, Colo.: Westview Press.

McNeely, J. A., and D. Pitt. 1985. *Culture and conservation: The human dimension in environmental planning*. London: Croom Helm.

Messier, Francois. 1993. *Moose management in Northern Quebec: Simulation scenarios and co-management*. Montreal: Report to the Grand Council of the Crees (of Quebec).

Osherenko, G. 1988. Sharing power with native users: Co-management regimes for native wildlife. Policy Paper No. 5. Ottawa: Canadian Arctic Resources Committee.

Pinkerton, E. 1989. Attaining better fisheries management through co-management: Prospects, problems, and propositions. In *Cooperative management of local fisheries*, E. Pinkerton, ed. 3–33. Vancouver: University of British Columbia Press.

Power, G. 1979. Problems of fisheries management in northern Quebec. *Fisheries Management* 10: 101–109.

Richardson, B. 1976. *Strangers devour the land*. New York: Alfred Knopf.

Richardson, B., ed. 1989. *Drumbeat: Anger and renewal in Indian country*. Toronto: Summerhill Press and the Assembly of First Nations.

Scott, C. H. 1982. Production and exchange among Wemindji Cree: Egalitarian ideology and economic base. *Culture* 2: 51–64.

Scott, C. H. 1984. Between "original affluence" and consumer affluence: Domestic production and guaranteed income for James Bay Cree hunters. In *Affluence and cultural survival*, R. F. Salisbury, ed. Washington, D.C.: American Ethnological Society.

Scott, C. H. 1987. The socio-economic significance of waterfowl among Canada's aboriginal Cree: Native use and local management. In *The value of birds*, A. N. Diamond and F. L. Filion, eds. Technical Publication No. 6. 49–62. Cambridge, United Kingdom: International Council for Bird Preservation.

Scott, C. H. 1991. Property, practice and aboriginal rights among Quebec Cree hunters. In *Hunters and gatherers 2: Property, power and ideology*, T. Ingold, D. Riches, and J. Woodburn, eds. 35–51. Oxford, United Kingdom: Berg.

Tanner, A. 1979. *Bringing home animals: Religious ideology and mode of production of the Mistassini Cree hunters*. St. John's: Memorial University Institute of Social and Economic Research.

Usher, P. J. 1981. Sustenance or recreation? The future of native wildlife harvesting in northern Canada. In *Renewable resources and the economy of the north*. M. M. R. Freeman, ed. 56–71. Ottawa: Association of Canadian Universities for Northern Studies and Man and Biosphere Program.

Usher, P. J. 1984. Property rights: The basis of wildlife management. In *National and regional interests in the north*. 389–415. Ottawa: Canadian Arctic Resources Committee.

Usher, P. J. 1986. The devolution of wildlife management and the prospects for wildlife conservation in the northwest territories. Policy Paper No. 3. Ottawa: Canadian Arctic Resources Committee.

Worl, R. 1980. The north slope Inupiat whaling complex. In *Alaska native culture and history*, Y. Kotani and W.B. Workman, eds. Senri Ethnological Studies, Osaka: National Museum of Ethnology.

CHAPTER NINE

INDIGENOUS PEOPLES: MISSING LINKS AND LOST KNOWLEDGE
IN THE CONSERVATION OF BRAZIL'S TROPICAL FORESTS

Darrell A. Posey

For decades many environmentalists have acted as though preservation
of nature had nothing to do with protecting humans, who were often seen as in-
nately destructive and in absolute opposition to conservation plans. Most experienced conservationists have now discovered, however, that unless people have a
direct stake and interest in these plans, conservation projects stand little chance for
long-term success (see *Caring for the Earth*, IUCN et al. 1993).

Today's rapid destruction of tropical forests can be partially attributed to
the lack of importance given to the traditional knowledge that native cultures have
of both the economic and ecological riches of tropical forests as well as to non-
natives' lack of knowledge of how to use the forests' vast diversity of medicines,
foods, natural fertilizers, and pesticides. In Amazonia today, tropical forests are
valued mostly for the economic benefits that cattle, lumber, and gold provide—
all of them attained through forest destruction. Indigenous peoples can teach us
how to give greater value to the *living* tropical forest, but only if they are given
equal status in the future of this planet. Unfortunately, accepting that native peoples
have much to teach us—via their own linguistic and conceptual frames of reference—seems one of the hardest lessons that modern society must learn. Because
colonizing societies have historically used cultural differences to justify imposing
their versions of progress and civilization to exploit indigenous lands and natural
resources, we have inherited a profoundly difficult problem.

Ethnobiology in the Defense of Native Peoples

Ethnobiology combines the multidisciplinary forces of Western cultural
traditions in order to document, study, and give value to the knowledge systems of
native peoples. Ethnobiologists present indigenous peoples not as exotic creatures
with strange cultural habits, but as societies that for millennia have lived in close
association with their environments. Recent archaeological evidence indicates that
indigenous peoples have been living in South America for perhaps as many as

35,000 years. Furthermore, researchers are finding that many presumed "natural" ecological systems in Amazonia are, in fact, products of human manipulation (Frikel 1959; Alcorn 1981, 1989; Anderson and Posey 1985; Balée 1989a, 1989b; Balée and Gely 1989; Posey and Balée 1989; Clement 1989). For example, ethnohistorical research has provided evidence that indigenous peoples came into contact with European diseases long before having direct contact with Europeans. There is evidence that these epidemics led to intragroup fighting and fission that, in turn, had recognizable effects on biological species dispersal. In the 19th century, indigenous people developed a form of "nomadic agriculture" to cultivate many domesticated and semidomesticated plant species in managed environments near trail sides, abandoned villages, and campsites. As a result, seeds, tubers, and cuttings were spread over vast areas to ensure the availability of valuable medicinal and edible species (Posey 1985).

In Brazil, the Kayapó Indians of Para State's Xingu Basin (Figure 9.1) have been an integral part of the Amazon ecosystem for thousands of years. Like other indigenous Amazonian peoples, their influence on the ecosystem has been and continues to be significant, although Western science has largely ignored both their knowledge of and impact on the region's biodiversity. More than three-fourths of the plant species used by the Kayapó, for example, are neither "domesticated" nor "wild," but have been systematically selected for desirable traits and propagated in a variety of habitats such as old fallows. Historically, during times of warfare, the Kayapó could abandon their agricultural plots and survive on these semidomesticated species that had been scattered in known spots throughout the forest and neighboring savanna. Old agricultural field sites thus became hunting reserves, and if properly planted, such old fields could develop into productive agroforestry plots dominated by semidomesticated species, allowing the Kayapó to shift between being agriculturists and hunter-gatherers. Such patterns, which appear to have been widespread throughout the lowland tropics, make archaic the traditional dichotomies of wild versus domesticated species, hunter-gatherers versus agriculturists, and agriculture versus agroforestry.

One of the major lessons learned from research in the last decade is that many apparently "natural" landscapes in Amazonia may actually be the result of human activity. However, far too many biologists and ecologists still ignore the archaeological, historical, anthropological, and ethnobiological literature linking biodiversity with the ways of indigenous peoples like the Kayapó. An understanding and appreciation of this indigenous knowledge is crucial for the preservation of these peoples as well as the forest itself. My studies of the Kayapó, for example, reveal that their ancient traditions—developed through millennia of experience, observation, and experiment—are extremely relevant to providing future options for sustainable natural resource management.

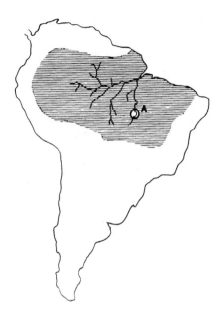

Figure 9.1. The Kayapó Indians inhabit the Xingu River Basin in the state of Para in Brazil (A). The Xingu is a tributary of the Amazon. (Amazon Basin shaded.)

Lessons from the Kayapó

When I started my research with the Kayapó Indians in 1977, I began to understand why it is easier to mount campaigns to save exotic species than it is to salvage endangered peoples. My first lesson came when I went to the Xingu River Indian Post of Kokraimoro. There had been little meat in the village for some time, and the Indians were eager to kill some game animals. They invited me to partici-pate in a hunting trip. After a long day in the forest, we were fortunate to kill a sizeable tapir and bring back a large hunk of meat. The Indians processed the meat by rubbing it with salt and storing it in a bowl of brackish water in the dark storage room of the cabin in which we were staying. When the residents left to go downriver, promising to return within two days, they asked me to keep an eye on things. After five days, I was still alone in the cabin. When I decided to look at our meat, I discovered to my horror that it was covered with fly maggots. I quickly threw out the noxious mess. Several Indians from a neighboring cabin passed by, saw the meat being thrown away, looked at me strangely, and asked for the meat—which I gladly gave them—and meandered off, looking quite pleased. I was puzzled as to why. The next day, my hosts returned from their prolonged journey. They were hungry for tapir meat and immediately asked about the prepared piece. When I informed them that I had thrown it out, they were very angry and even threatened to throw me out of the cabin.

It seems that some maggots exude enzymes that help break down the more gristly parts of meat. One has only to remove the maggots with a good washing and place the meat in the sun in order to have a nice tender piece. Still, I could not help but think, "Who would want to live with people who eat such horrible things?" It was not until I confronted my own prejudices and Western ideals of "cleanliness" and "civilization" that I could begin to appreciate how much I had to learn from these people and their ways.

Kayapó Indian knowledge is an integrated system of beliefs and practices. Each Kayapó believes that he or she has the ability to survive alone in the forest indefinitely, and this philosophy offers great personal security and permeates the fabric of everyday life. In addition to the information shared generally, each village has its specialist in soils, plants, animals, crops, medicines, and rituals. A complete Kayapó view of nature is difficult to convey because of its underlying cultural complexity. It is useful, however, to identify categories of indigenous knowledge that may indicate important research directions for Western science as well as provide alternatives to the destruction of Amazonia.

Ecology

The Kayapó identify plants and animals according to particular ecological zones, each zone representing a system of interactions among plants, animals, soils, and the Kayapó themselves. Similarly, ecosystems are believed to lie on a continuum between the poles of forest and savanna. The Kayapó have names for as many as nine different types of savanna—savanna with few trees, savanna with many forest patches, savanna with scrub, and so on. Yet they concentrate less on the differences among these zones than on the similarities they share. Marginal or open spots in the forest can have microenvironmental conditions similar to those in the savanna, for example, and the Kayapó exchange and spread useful species among zones by transplanting seeds, cuttings, tubers, and saplings. By exploiting secondary forest areas and creating special concentrations of plants in fields within the forest, rock outcroppings, and trailsides, the Kayapó actually create what we refer to as "ecotones" (Posey 1985). There is also a considerable degree of interchange among what we tend to see as distinctly different ecological systems.

The creation of forest islands, or Apêtê, demonstrates the extent to which the Kayapó can alter and manage ecosystems to increase biological diversity. In creating these "islands of forest" in the campo-cerrado, the Kayapó have concentrated in one 10-hectare plot plant varieties collected from an area the size of Western Europe (Anderson and Posey 1989).

Apêtê begin as small mounds of vegetation, about one to two meters around, created by mixing organic matter from termite and ant nests to fill depressions in the savanna. Slight depressions are preferred because they are more likely to retain moisture. The Kayapó then plant seedlings in these piles of organic material. Usually they form the Apêtê in August and September, during the first rains of the wet season, and nurture the mounds as they pass along the savanna trails.

As the Apêtê grow, they begin to look like upturned hats, with higher vegetation in the center and lower herbs growing in the shaded borders. The Kayapó usually cut down the highest trees in the center to create a doughnut-hole center that lets in more light. Thus a full-grown Apêtê has zones that vary in shade, light, and humidity. These islands have become important sources of medicinal and edible plants as well as places of rest. Palms, which have a variety of uses, figure prominently in Apêtê as do shade trees and vines that produce drinking water. Apêtê look so natural, that until recently Western scientists did not recognize that they were made by humans. According to Kayapó interviews, about 75 percent of 120 species inventoried in 10 Apêtê could have been planted (Anderson and Posey 1989). Such ecological engineering requires detailed knowledge of soil fertility, microclimatic variations, and species' niches as well as the interrelationships among species that are introduced into these human-made biological communities. In addition to their knowledge of forest plants, the Kayapó have a well-developed knowledge of animal behavior and the associations among plants and animals. The eating habits of deer and tapir are well known, for example, and their favorite foods are propagated in forest islands to attract the game. The forest islands must thus be viewed as both agroforestry plots and hunting reserves.

Like the Apêtê, Kayapó fields thrive on diversity. The Kayapó are aware that some plant species develop more vigorously when planted together. For example, they frequently speak of plants that are "good friends" or "good neighbors," such as the tyryti-õmbiqua, or "banana neighbors." Among the plants that thrive near bananas are the mẽkraketdjà ("child want not") plants, which are important in regulating human fertility. The Kayapó characterize such synergistic plant groups—which can include dozens of species and require complex patterns of cultivation—in terms of "plant energy." A Kayapó garden is created by carefully combining different plant energies just as an artist blends colors to produce a work of art. Kayapó fields may look a "mess" to Westerners who are conditioned to "clean" fields with orderly, symmetrical rows. But what may appear to us as random field plantings are quite ordered to the Kayapó eye. They include five concentric zones, each with preferred varieties of cultivars and different cultivation strategies.

Botany and Pharmacology

The Kayapó classify plants based on each species' pharmacological properties or ability to treat disease. While these plant categories cut across morphologically-based botanical groupings, they nevertheless exhibit a high degree of correlation with Western botanical classification. Almost every Kayapó household has its complement of common medicinal plants, many of them domesticates or semidomesticates. Rare medicinal plants are often brought from distant areas and transplanted near homes or in special medicinal rock gardens. Other useful plants are managed in a similar way. "Kupa" (*Cissus gongylodes*), for instance, is an edible domesticate known only to the Kayapó and some of their kin. An estimated 250 plants are used for their fruits alone. In addition, the Kayapó classify more than 150 types of diarrhea and dysentery, each of which is treated with specific medicines. Ethnopharmacologists and physicians frequently forget that disease categories are intellectually perceived phenomena that can be culturally classified.

Zoology

Another important aspect of the Kayapó's ecological knowledge begins at a very early age when children are encouraged to learn the behavior patterns and feeding habits of different animal species. Part of this knowledge is gained through rearing pets; in a survey conducted with tropical biologist Kent Redford, we found more than 60 species of birds, reptiles, snakes, amphibians, mammals— even spiders—being raised in one village. Over the years, the children grow to be astute observers of animal behavior and anatomy, skills that are important in hunting, agriculture, and even medicine.

For example, the Kayapó deliberately place nests of "smelly ants" (of the genus *Azteca*) in gardens and on fruit trees that are infested with leaf-cutter ants (*Atta* spp.) because the pheromones of the "smelly ants" repel the leaf-cutters. These protective ants are also prized for their medicinal properties and are frequently crushed for their highly aromatic scents, which, when inhaled, open up stuffy sinuses. The Kayapó also cultivate several plants that contain extrafloral nectaries, which attract predatory ants that serve as "bodyguards" for the plants. Banana trees, for example, are often planted to form a living wall around their fields because predatory wasps prefer to nest under the leaves. Stingless bees (Meliponidae) are one of the Kayapó's most valued insect resources. During the dry season, groups of men frequently go off for days to find honey, which they drink at the collection site. Beeswax is then brought back to the village to be burned in ceremonies and used in many artifacts. Shamans who specialize in curing bites and stings of certain animals (such as snakes, lizards, and scorpions) become experts on the behavior of these animals. Through their day-to-day experiences, the Kayapó have thus accumulated a vast amount of information about many animals and plants that Western scientists still consider little-known species (Posey 1986).

Soils, Agriculture, and Agroforestry

The Kayapó knowledge of soil taxonomy is also very sophisticated. They make horizontal and vertical distinctions in the soil based on qualities such as texture, color, drainage, friability, and stratification (Hecht and Posey 1989). In addition, soil qualities are related to indicator plant species that allow the Kayapó to predict floral and faunal components associated with specific soil types, each of which is managed differently. Sweet potatoes, for instance, prefer hotter soil and thrive in the center of fields where shade from the margins rarely penetrates. These plants must be well aerated or soil compaction will smother the root system. Hard work is therefore devoted to turning over the soils, taking out larger tubers, and replanting smaller ones.

The Kayapó also use various types of ground cover such as vegetation, logs, leaves, straw, and bark to affect the moisture, shade, and temperature of local soils. They often fill holes with organic matter, refuse, and ash to produce highly concentrated pockets of rich soil. In addition, old banana leaves, stalks, rice straw, and other organic matter are piled and sometimes burned in parts of fields to create additional local variation of micronutrients. The Kayapó have dozens of types of plant ash, each said to have certain qualities preferred by specific cultivars. The ash is usually prepared from the vines, shucks, stalks, and leaves of plants that have been cut or uprooted during harvesting or weeding. Sometimes piles of organic matter are made, with the different varieties carefully separated and allowed to dry in the sun until they will give a complete burn. They then distribute the ashes to the appropriate part of the field.

The Kayapó do not make a clear distinction between fields and forest or between wild and domesticated species. Gathered plants are transplanted into concentrated spots near trails and campsites to produce "forest fields," and the sides of trails themselves are planting zones. It is not uncommon, therefore, to find trails composed of four-meter-wide cleared strips of forest. This process of domestication, frequently assumed to be ancient, still occurs thanks to indigenous groups like the Kayapó, who have selected literally hundreds of plant varieties and planted them in human-modified ecological systems. Similar activities by other indigenous peoples continue throughout the Amazon.

The Kayapó design their agricultural plots to be productive through a cycle of reforestation in which useful species are introduced to a forest opening. This strategy creates a mature forest of concentrated resources, including game animals. Contrary to persistent beliefs about indigenous slash-and-burn agriculture, these fields are *not* abandoned after a few years of use following initial clearing and planting. On the contrary, old fields retain an important concentration of diverse resources long after primary cultivars are gone. Although the fields peak in production of principal domesticated crops in two or three years, they continue to bear produce for many more—sweet potatoes for four to five years, yams and taro for five to six years, papaya and banana for five or more years. The Kayapó consistently revisit old fields seeking these lingering riches (Posey 1985).

Traditional Knowledge and Rain Forest Harvests

Industry and business discovered many years ago that indigenous knowledge means money. In the earliest forms of colonialism, products extracted from forests and other habitats formed the basis of colonial wealth. More recently, pharmaceutical industries have become the major exploiters of traditional medicinal knowledge for major products and profits. The annual world-market value for medicines derived from plants discovered from indigenous peoples may be upwards of U.S.$40 billion (see Posey 1987, 1994a,b).

Although no comparable figures are published for natural insecticides, insect repellents, and plant genetic materials acquired from native peoples, the annual monetary potential for these products is also astounding. Research into these natural products is only beginning, with projections of their market values exceeding all other tropical forest food and medicinal products combined. The international seed industry alone accounts for more than $15 billion per year. Likewise, natural fragrances, dyes, and body and hair products from developing countries are gaining major world markets, often sold as products obtained through ecologically sustainable projects managed by native peoples themselves.

This growing interest in "natural" food, and medicinal, agricultural, and cosmetic products has spawned an increase in research into traditional knowledge systems. Now, more than ever, the intellectual-property rights of native peoples must be protected and just compensation for knowledge guaranteed. We cannot simply rely upon the "good will" of companies and institutions to "do right by" indigenous peoples. If something is not done now, mining of the riches of indigenous knowledge will become the latest—and ultimate—neocolonial form of exploitation. Provocations of cultural changes can be equally disconcerting. By establishing mechanisms for "just compensation," for example, are we not also establishing mechanisms for the destruction of native societies through materialism and consumerism?

Today, indigenous societies and their natural environments are being rapidly destroyed by the expansion of industrialized society. Pharmaceutical companies and "natural products" companies have already tasted the success of their efforts, and they are sure to exert even more pressure on indigenous societies in the coming decades. As the production of "natural products" becomes more financially rewarding, many ecologists warn that this success will inevitably lead to monocultures of cash crops and that international demands may promote the destruction of biodiversity rather than encourage conservation of natural resources (Soulé and Kohm 1989).

Traditional knowledge provides some of the missing links necessary in conserving tropical ecosystems. Yet we are far from having the sophistication needed to deal with the scientific value of knowledge that comes from our "primitive" neighbors. We are even less willing to find ways of sharing with them the economic fruits of our societies or even those "harvested" from their own indigenous knowledge systems. Native peoples must have the right to choose their own futures. Without economic independence, such a choice is not possible. The current devastation of native peoples and the ecological systems that they have conserved, managed, and intimately known for millennia require new and drastic steps to reorient world priorities. All channels and organizations—governmental, nongovernmental, professional, business—must work together to reverse the world's accelerating loss of cultural, ecological, and biological diversity.

Epilogue

Reflecting on the changes that have occurred since I wrote the original of this chapter several years ago, I am reminded of the huge amount of time, energy, and effort that went into the 1992 Earth Summit. More than 150 heads of state signed the Convention on Biological Diversity (CBD) and the Declaration of Rio de Janeiro.

The Declaration (Principle 22) clearly establishes the central importance of indigenous peoples to sustainable development:

Indigenous people and their communities, and other local communities, have a vital role in environmental management and development because of their knowledge and traditional practices. States should recognize and duly support their identity, culture and interests and enable their effective participation in the achievement of sustainable development.

Likewise, Article 8 (j) of the Convention pledges that signatories will:

respect, preserve and maintain knowledge, innovations, and practices of indigenous and local communities embodying traditional lifestyles relevant for the conservation and sustainable use of biological diversity and promote their wider application with the approval and involvement of the holders of such knowledge, innovations and practices and encourage the equitable sharing of the benefits arising from the utilization of such knowledge, innovations and practices.

Still, indigenous groups doubt that existing international and national laws will adequately recognize and protect their knowledge, innovations, and practices. They are skeptical that "trickle-down benefits" will occur, since historically they have rarely benefited from the goodwill of nation-states. They are particularly concerned that their rights to self-determination will be further undermined by loss of control over their cultural, scientific, and intellectual property. Indigenous peoples have discovered that even guaranteed demarcation of land and territory does not necessarily mean guaranteed access to resources on that land or territory, nor even the right to exercise their own culture or be compensated for the biogenetic resources that they have kept, conserved, managed, and molded within local ecosystems for millennia (see Posey 1994b).

Increasingly, "biodiversity prospectors" enter indigenous lands to "discover" potential new medicines, oils, essences, insecticides, repellents, dyes, foods, hair conditioners, and natural fertilizers. Yet despite the international hype of the CBD, few countries are even considering the recognition of native rights to protection of and compensation for their knowledge and biogenetic resources.

Historically, links between local communities and distant markets—especially international ones—have had disastrous effects for indigenous peoples. Environmentalists also point out that commercializing natural products often has deleterious effects on the environment. Thus, the fundamental questions of how to maintain biological and cultural diversity through the sustainable use of biological diversity and equitable use of traditional knowledge remain unanswered. Meanwhile, the destruction accelerates.

Acknowledgments

I wrote all but the epilogue of this paper while I was a fellow of the Alexander von Humboldt Foundation at the Zoologische Staatssammlung in Munich, Germany. I would like to thank the Foundation and my host institution for the opportunity and freedom to work on this and other papers. A portion of this paper was published in *Orion Nature Quarterly*.

In 1982, I initiated a multidisciplinary ethnobiological project called the Kayapó Project that eventually included more than 20 scientists and technicians from different scientific fields such as agronomy, botany, entomology, plant genetics, astronomy, geography, anthropology, and linguistics in an effort to document the traditional biological knowledge of the Kayapó Indians of Para State, Brazil. My ethnobiological research with the Kayapó began in 1977 with initial grants from the Wenner-Gren Foundation for Anthropological Research. The multidisciplinary Kayapó Project was funded for its first two years (1982-83) by the Brazilian Council for Science and Technology (CNPQ). Since 1984, the Project had received financial aid from: WWF-US (general enthnobiological investigation), WWF-International (research and education), the National Geographic Society (mapping and ethnoecological zone definition), and the Ford Foundation-Brazil (ethnobiological training).

References Cited

Alcorn, J. B. 1981. Huastec noncrop resource management: Implications for prehistoric rain forest management. *Human Ecology* 9: 395–417.

Alcorn, J. B. 1989. Process as resource: The traditional agricultural ideology of Bora and Huastec resource management and its implications for research. In *Resource management in Amazonia: Indigenous and folk strategies*, D. Posey and W. Balée, eds. *Advances in Economic Botany* 7: 63–77.

Anderson, A. B. and D. A. Posey. 1985. Manejo de Cerrado pelos Indios Kayapó. *Boletim do Museu Paraense Emílio Goeldi Botanica* 2: 77–98.

Anderson, A. B., and D. A. Posey. 1989. Management of tropical scrub savanna by the Gorotire Kayapó of Brazil. In *Resource management in Amazonia: Indigenous and folk strategies*, D. Posey and W. Balée, eds. *Advances in Economic Botany* 7: 159–172.

Balée, W. L. 1989a. The culture of Amazonian forests. In *Resource management in Amazonia: Indigenous and folk strategies*, D. Posey and W. Balée ed. *Advances in Economic Botany*, 7: 1–21.

Balée, W. L. 1989b. Cultura na vegetação da Amazonia. *Boletim do Museu Paraense Emílio Goeldi, Coleção Eduardo Galvão* 1: 95–109.

Balée, W. L., and A. Gely. 1989. Managed forest succession in Amazonia: The Ka'apor Case. In *Resource management in Amazonia: Indigenous and folk strategies*, D. Posey and W. Balée, eds. *Advances in Economic Botany* 7: 129–148.

Clement, C. R. 1989. A center of crop genetic diversity in Western Amazonia: A new hypothesis of indigenous fruit–crop distribution. *Bioscience* 39: 624–630.

Frikel, P. 1959. Agricultura dos Indios Mundurucu. *Boletim do Museu Paraense Emílio Goeldi, Serie Anthropolica*, 8: 1–41.

Hecht, S. B., and D. A. Posey. 1989. Preliminary results on soil management techniques of the Kayapó Indians. In *Resource management in Amazonia: Indigenous and folk strategies*, D. Posey and W. Balée, eds. *Advances in Economic Botany* 7: 174–188.

International Union for the Conservation of Nature, United Nations Environmental Programme, and World Wildlife Fund. *Caring for the earth: A strategy for sustainable living*. 1993. Produced by the International Union for the Conservation of Nature, the United Nations Education Programme, and World Wildlife Fund. Melbourne: Reed International Books.

Posey, D. A. 1985. Indigenous management of tropical forest ecosystems: The case of the Kayapó Indians of the Brazilian Amazon. *Agroforestry Systems* 3: 139–158.

Posey, D. A. 1986. Topics and issues in ethnoentomology with some suggestions for the development of hypothesis-generation and testing in ethnobiology. *Journal of Ethnobiology* 6: 99–120.

Posey, D. A. 1987. Contact before contact: Typology of post-Columbian interaction with Northern Kayapó of the Amazon Basin. *Boletim do Museu Paraense Emílio Goeldi, Serie Antropologica* 3: 135–154.

Posey, D. A. 1994a. Environmental and social implications of the pre- and postcontact situations on Brazilian Indians: the Kayapó and a new Amazonian synthesis. In *Amazonian Indians from prehistory to the present: Anthropological perspectives*, Anna Roosevelt, ed. Tucson: University of Arizona Press.

Posey, D. A. 1994b. International agreements and intellectual property right protection for indigenous peoples. In *Intellectual property rights for indigenous peoples: A source book*, Thomas Greaves, ed. 223–252. Oklahoma City: Society for Applied Anthropology.

Posey, D. A., and W. Balée, eds. 1989. Resource management in Amazonia: Indigenous and folk strategies. In *Advances in Economic Botany* 7. New York: New York Botanic Gardens.

Soulé, M. E., and K. A. Kohm. 1989. *Research priorities for conservation biology*. Washington, D.C.: Island Press.

CHAPTER TEN

THE ALLIANCE BETWEEN THE INDIGENOUS PEOPLES OF THE
AMAZON BASIN AND ENVIRONMENTAL ORGANIZATIONS IN
NORTH AMERICA

Stewart J. Hudson

In October 1989, representatives of North American environmental groups met in Washington, D.C., with representatives of indigenous peoples of the Amazon Basin to explore the possibility of forming an alliance. That meeting and two others held the following year led to the creation of a formal alliance between several U.S. and Canadian environmental organizations and the Coordinating Body for the Indigenous Peoples Organizations of the Amazon Basin (COICA).

To understand the relevance of the alliance, particularly its importance to discussions of the connections between culture and conservation, one must first know something about the organization known as COICA and the reasons it was founded. This chapter begins by explaining COICA and then provides a description and analysis of the three meetings that laid the groundwork for the alliance. It concludes with a commentary on how the alliance might serve to further both the preservation of cultural diversity and the conservation of natural resources in the Amazon Basin. Material is drawn from COICA documents and interviews with COICA representatives, as well as from news articles, interviews with environmentalists, and my own participation in two meetings. However, this personal account should in no way be interpreted as representing COICA's side of the story, nor should it be characterized as the environmentalist position on the alliance, as there exists a diversity of opinion on this subject.

What Is COICA?

Founded in Lima, Peru, in March 1984, COICA's goal is to represent the interests of indigenous peoples living in the Amazon Basin through a network of national, regional, and local indigenous organizations. In 1989 the organization had members representing five Amazon Basin countries: the Confederation of Indigenous Communities and Peoples of Eastern Bolivia; the Union of Indigenous Nations in Brazil; the National Organization of Indigenous Peoples of Colombia; the Confederation of Indigenous Nationalities of the Ecuadorian Amazon; and the

Inter-ethnic Association for Development of the Peruvian Jungle. Together these COICA members represent almost 200 different indigenous groups in the Amazon Basin (COICA 1988a). As stated by the organization, COICA's objectives are:

- to defend our rights as indigenous peoples as well as members of the human community, and to defend our territories and our self-determination;
- to represent member organizations in international meetings and in forums with governmental and non-governmental organizations;
- to strengthen the unity of all indigenous peoples;
- to promote indigenous cultural values through a process of autonomous development within each country;
- to incorporate into our organization any interested indigenous peoples in the process of organizing themselves at a national level (COICA 1988a).

Historical Perspective

The historical process that led to COICA's formation began in the late 1970s, when indigenous groups throughout the Amazon began organizing themselves into regional and, in some cases, national organizations. While these organizations made several important advances, many were undermined by decisions made at an international level. World Bank hydroelectric projects, for example, flooded huge tracts of Indian land, and their associated road projects promoted colonization of indigenous lands by outsiders. Without the participation of indigenous peoples or their leaders, both the Organization of American States and United Nations made policy decisions unfavorable to indigenous groups. All of these problems contributed to COICA's creation and the organization's demand to participate in international meetings dealing with indigenous issues.

Another goal of COICA has been to correct a popular image of indigenous people as unwilling and incapable of adapting to the modern world—that they are exotic and meant to be preserved as such. According to COICA president Evaristo Nukguag, "Museum anthropologists often present indigenous peoples as if they were animals in a zoological garden" (Hudson 1989). COICA also promotes the right of indigenous peoples to decide for themselves what their image should be, rather than leaving that interpretation to outsiders such as anthropologists, environmentalists, and human-rights activists.

COICA also strives to ensure that indigenous people are treated as human beings and "members of the community." While this concern might seem strange at first, for the indigenous peoples of the Amazon, their "humanness" is anything but assured. In Colombia, for example, charges of homicide have been dismissed against rural colonists because they did not believe that killing Indians was the same as murder. In Peru, enslavement of one Amazonian tribe is believed to still exist (COICA 1989a). In addition to this abuse, a more subtle type of racism is often found in the paternalism with which many indigenous people are treated. They are either placed on a pedestal and idealized as the noble savage, or they are seen as victims, robbed of the right to decide their own future.

Today most conversation about COICA's objectives begins with a call to support indigenous land claims. COICA leaders argue that economic security and cultural survival are embedded in securing land rights and that the recognition of indigenous land claims will be more effective than the establishment of national parks in achieving conservation goals.

A Possible Alliance

It was not until late 1989 that COICA's leaders first voiced the possibility of an alliance with North American environmentalists. To explore this idea, they proposed that a meeting be held on October 19, 1989, in Washington, D.C. Their letter of invitation stated that the purpose of the meeting would be "...to discuss a possible alliance of equals with the North American environmental movement" (COICA 1989b).

To facilitate discussion at the meeting, COICA prepared and distributed a document entitled "To the Community of Concerned Environmentalists," which laid out its position on several issues. Although it began by commending U.S. environmental groups for their lobbying activities, it moved quickly to a targeted criticism of these same organizations. COICA's first and most strident criticism of the environmental community was that it failed to consider the real interests of the Amazon's indigenous peoples. From COICA's viewpoint, the U.S. environmental community considered conservation more important than the welfare of the Amazonian Indians. The organization also took U.S. environmental groups to task for speaking on behalf of indigenous peoples without their consent or approval.

COICA specifically criticized debt-for-nature swaps—arrangements by which a small portion of a developing country's external debt is retired in return for a commitment to use a portion of the funds saved for conservation purposes. COICA argued that the swaps "put the environmentalists in the position of negotiating with [their] governments the future of [their] homelands." In particular, COICA criticized a debt-for-nature swap that had been launched in Bolivia, saying that it served as an example of "how these swaps can happen with the most brazen disregard for the rights of indigenous inhabitants and result in the ultimate destruction of the very forests which the swap was meant to preserve" (COICA 1988b).

At the October 1989, meeting, COICA reiterated these criticisms and argued that recognition of indigenous land rights would be a more effective conservation measure than trying to protect land set aside as parks and reserves. Several members of the environmental community rose to defend debt-for-nature swaps, while acknowledging some of the difficulties inherent in their implementation. After a heated discussion, the meeting turned to a consideration of COICA's participation in international forums. Since 1984, COICA had made some headway in this area, participating in United Nations and International Labor Organization debates about indigenous human-rights issues. In 1986, they had met with the president of the World Bank and senior officials of the Inter-American Development Bank to discuss their concerns about bank projects in the Amazon Basin. The meeting with World Bank president Barber Conable generated media attention for COICA in the United States.

By 1989, however, it was environmentalists in the North who had received the most media attention for their protests against multilateral development banks. Because COICA clearly wanted to be part of the action, it expressed its desire at the October meeting to be more involved in decisions made by multilateral institutions. The organization again criticized environmentalists for speaking as if they represented indigenous peoples. As stated more succinctly in an earlier publication, COICA insisted that only its own members "...represent themselves and [their] interests in all negotiations concerning the future of our Amazonian homeland" (COICA 1988b).

To many environmental groups, this was a curious complaint given the efforts that many of them had made to pressure banks to include indigenous peoples in project selection, design, and implementation. Despite these efforts, COICA clearly felt left out of the process. The meeting closed with an agreement that a formal alliance should be formed, and a subsequent meeting was scheduled for early 1990 in Iquitos, Peru.

"Rumble in the Rain Forest"

The purpose of the Iquitos meeting, to make "...concrete agreements for the formation of an alliance for the defense of the Amazon," proved to be deeply frustrating to both sides (COICA 1990a). Environmentalists who attended were greeted by a background document that represented COICA's "position." The document began with a description of COICA's concerns about Indian land rights, and again put forth the proposition that sound conservation of the natural resources of the Amazon Basin is impossible without securing these rights. The document concluded by calling on environmental groups to work with COICA to reclaim and conserve indigenous territories "as an effective proposal for [their] common objective...to create a better future for the Amazon and mankind" (COICA 1990c).

There was little in the document that environmentalists had not heard at the Washington meeting. What may have got the Iquitos meeting off to a bad start, however, was COICA's insistence that environmentalists respond by stating their "position." According to many of the environmentalists present, this demand was difficult to understand. It was unclear whether they were being asked to state a common position on the idea of having an alliance or on indigenous peoples' issues in general. Even if they had understood what was being asked, they were not prepared to come up with a consensus without previous consultation among themselves.

In retrospect, it is clear that there were two very different expectations as to what was to be produced in Iquitos. COICA hoped to be able to receive political endorsements for a host of issues ranging from general indigenous land rights to the abolition of slavery in the Amazon Basin. Environmental groups, however, did not expect to have to deal with these issues in a formal way, and despite personal agreement with COICA's positions, few had an organizational mandate to address the entire range of problems indigenous people face. The realization that there was no unified "environmental position" was very frustrating to COICA.

After this rocky start, the second day of the meeting began with what was intended to be a brief discussion of the debt issue, including consideration of both debt-for-nature swaps and COICA's proposal for debt for indigenous territory. COICA representatives argued that North American environmental groups, in concert with Amazon Basin governments, were secretly negotiating away indigenous land rights. They also pointed out that the commercial timber harvest had actually accelerated in the area of Bolivia where Conservation International had negotiated the most celebrated debt-for-nature swap so far. Some conservationists, particularly those involved with the Bolivian swap, counterargued that environmental degradation had not accelerated and that the swap had actually encouraged more rational use of resources in the area. They also insisted that the swap had been initiated in consultation with some of the local indigenous groups and that the differences among these indigenous groups—rather than a failure to consult with them—lay behind the criticisms. The discussion, expected to last a few hours, ran the entire day and ended inconclusively.

Participants spent the final day of the Iquitos meeting hammering out a common accord that would later be known as the Iquitos Declaration. This, too, was a frustrating process for both sides. COICA felt that, as individuals, all participants could endorse recommendations such as campaigns for specific land claims and the abolition of slavery in the Amazon Basin. But COICA did not understand the apolitical nature of some groups attending, nor did they realize that most attendees could not commit their organizations to important new policies without some process of internal review—making it difficult to commit those organizations even to something as unimpeachable as an end to slavery.

Despite these misunderstandings, all the attendees wanted to come to some agreement as the basis for an alliance, and a smaller working group of COICA representatives and environmentalists was able to draft a common statement. The Iquitos Declaration was unanimously endorsed by all groups present—a notable achievement in itself. Its first clause stated that "recognition of territories for indigenous people, to develop programs of management and conservation, is an essential alternative for the future of the Amazon" (COICA 1990b). According to Barbara Bramble, director of the National Wildlife Federation's International Programs, this clause represented a carefully crafted agreement in which both sides were able to extract something from the other. The indigenous representatives secured a commitment of support for their efforts to recover their territories. In return environmentalists won an emphasis on "management and conservation" (Hudson 1990a).

Other clauses in the Iquitos Declaration covered agreements on securing financial resources for the newly formed alliance as well as formal recognition of the importance of indigenous models of development. The document expressed support for projects that are consistent with "the proposals of COICA and...the particular objectives of each environmental and conservationist organization." It concluded by recognizing the formal alliance between environmentalists and COICA, stating that it is necessary to "continue working as an Indigenous and Environmentalist Alliance for an Amazon for Humanity."

The negative feelings stirred up in Iquitos and the watered-down nature of the declaration disappointed many participants. Yet public statements made after the meeting were positive. Joe Kane of the Rainforest Action Network, for example, stated that "to help save the Amazon, we will make securing land rights an important issue." Wilfrido Aragon of Ecuador, one of the COICA representatives most suspicious of environmentalists' motives, said: "We are all much more optimistic now because we are walking down the same path together" (Johnson 1990). These and similar positive statements set the stage for a follow-up meeting between COICA and U.S. environmentalists in Washington, D.C., in September 1990.

Second Meeting

The September 1990, meeting in Washington was by all accounts much more positive and productive than the Iquitos meeting. In contrast to the first meeting, fewer people attended and the press was not invited. Discussions did not degenerate into accusations and counterattacks, but instead evolved into a consideration of concrete actions to strengthen the newly formed alliance between environmentalists and indigenous peoples.

At the meeting's outset, participants agreed that subcommittees of alliance members would focus on problem areas in each of the five countries where COICA had members. These included:

- the issue of the Chimanes in Bolivia, one of the groups directly affected by activities of timber companies in the area of Conservation International's debt-for-nature swap;

- the Yanomami in Brazil, who had for some time been besieged by gold miners invading their lands;
- land rights of indigenous people in Pastaza, Ecuador;
- newly recovered indigenous territories in the Colombian Amazon;
- the creation of indigenous reserves in Peru.

In addition to the subcommittee work, participants agreed that the alliance would continue to address five major themes:

- recognition and recovery of indigenous territories;
- management of tropical forests;
- use rights and activities related to subsurface minerals;
- human rights, and social and political rights of indigenous people; and
- policies on protected areas.

Finally, the mechanics of planning for future alliance activities were discussed, and a work plan agreed upon. Several days after the official meetings, a smaller working group met to go over the meeting notes to ensure that they accurately represented what had taken place.

Commentary

The three alliance meetings have led to a greater trust between COICA and the North American environmental community. Before the meetings COICA representatives viewed environmentalists as the enemy, on a par with oil companies, timber interests, and land speculators who were threatening their land.

To be sure, some of this distrust had been justified. There are examples of environmental groups claiming to represent indigenous groups without ever having even consulted them. Others have routinely put their own institutional interests ahead of those of indigenous peoples. Through the alliance meetings, COICA representatives have become familiar with the idiosyncrasies of the international environmental movement and are less eager to maintain the image of environmentalists as adversarial. As many of the conflicts in Iquitos could be attributed to COICA's negative perception of all environmentalists, this change in perception is critical for the alliance to prosper. Similarly, the meetings made environmentalists aware of the absolute seriousness with which COICA approached each meeting and the issues discussed.

Despite the conflicts at the Iquitos meeting, it is very significant that the meeting did not self-destruct. Part of the reason may have been a sudden recognition that the alliance was too important to let go. For many environmentalists, an alliance with indigenous people is necessary to have any moral standing for their work on Amazonian issues. They also recognize that indigenous people have the greatest accumulated knowledge of how to live sustainably in the Amazon, and can provide some examples of alternatives to current irrational patterns of development. COICA, with its expanding representation of indigenous organizations, can help put conservation organizations in contact with these local people. Similarly, COICA benefits from the political power it gains by participating in an alliance with environmentalists as well as by increased access to funding and technical support for projects undertaken by its members.

The realization of these benefits for both sides should help the alliance survive the difficult steps it must take in the future. Thus far, almost all the demands made at the meetings have been made by indigenous peoples of environmentalists. What will happen when environmentalists begin to make demands of COICA or, in keeping with COICA's desire to be treated as equals, begin to challenge some of the assumptions COICA puts forth? Take, for example, COICA's position that indigenous peoples are in all cases the *best* defenders of the forest. Some environmental groups criticize this claim because they realize, quite correctly, that it would reduce their own influence in natural areas. A more legitimate criticism is that there are, and will continue to be, indigenous peoples who are neither willing nor able to manage their resources sustainably (Redford 1990). Many environmentalists also question whether indigenous people will be able to sustainably manage their land as economic incentives push them toward a market-oriented economy.

If the alliance can resolve some of its internal difficulties, it will become a powerful force promoting cultural preservation and natural resource conservation in the Amazon Basin. Results are already forthcoming. At the Iquitos meeting, for example, COICA learned that it had been recognized as the official representative for indigenous concerns before the Inter-Amazon Basin Commission, a commission formed by the Amazon Pact countries to deal with developmental and environmental issues. In Bolivia, COICA representatives are playing an important role in the implementation of a World Bank project. And in Montreal, during the annual meeting of the Inter-American Development Bank in 1990, COICA's Evaristo Nukguag delivered one of the keynote addresses at a seminar on the environment.

Prospects for the future can best be summarized by Wilfrido Aragon, formerly of the Ecuadorian counterpart of COICA. When asked what he has learned from dealing with the environmentalists who are part of this new alliance, he said:

> What I have is hope. It is not immediate. It is part of a process,
> that we are part of...a positive answer to the world, as to how the
> world can be reconstructed, as to how the world and the sacred
> and timeless things in it can be protected...[My hope is] drawn
> from the example of how indigenous people live in harmony
> with their natural surroundings (Hudson 1990b).

Epilogue

Since 1990, several changes have occurred in the nature of the alliance between COICA and North American conservation organizations. To some extent, the alliance has been overshadowed by COICA's broadened ties with conservation and human-rights groups in Europe. This has been especially true in terms of funding. Several European nongovernmental organizations as well as national and local governments have also provided political support.

The nature of conservation matters has also shifted since 1990. While there are still a number of conservation and human-rights issues that affect peoples of the Amazon Basin, global attention has drifted to other concerns. Headlines about the burning of the Amazon have been replaced by less dramatic reporting on other subjects such as the lack of conservation progress since the 1992 Earth Summit in Rio de Janeiro. As the glare of media attention on the environment has waned, there has also been less focus on the alliance between conservationists and indigenous peoples. This is a not entirely negative trend, however, and may be in part responsible for less posturing and more substantive work from those who still participate in the alliance.

Another new development is that COICA itself has gone through some significant leadership changes, which have shortened the ambitious list of goals presented by the organization in the late 1980s. With regard to leadership, COICA's new structure is much more decentralized and participatory. The position of the president has been eliminated, and in its place the organization now relies on coordinators of five basic thematic areas and a general coordinator to act as liaison with the other five. Participation has also grown; COICA's members now represent nine countries, with Guyana, Surinam, and Venezuela having joined as formal members. To reach out to this increased membership, the organization now publishes a newsletter and has an e-mail address.

While the leadership and other changes have been significant, they have strengthened rather than weakened the organization. COICA is clearly perceived as the only agency to speak for collective views of the indigenous peoples of the Amazon. It also continues to help channel funding for many of its member organizations and assists in implementing a variety of projects in the region.

On the political front, COICA members have successfully pressured their governments to respond more to their concerns. Within the region, COICA has gained increased clout with the Amazon Treaty Organization, which has invited it to participate in working groups and meetings on indigenous peoples and sustainable development in the Amazon. To increase its clout with governments and international organizations, COICA used various strategies including organized marches and protests and making the organization's views known through written and oral submissions to governments, the media, and international financial institutions.

Another indicator of success is that COICA and other local indigenous groups now clearly take the leadership on political issues and defining the agenda. In the past, the support provided by North American organizations often made it seem like they were leading the charge. Today, it is indigenous groups like COICA that chart the course of action, and while the alliance's conservation partners remain supportive, they do not change the direction of indigenous peoples' campaigns.

One final goal of the alliance, at least as defined in 1990, was to foster a greater intellectual understanding of the connection between culture and conservation. Here it is possible to credit the alliance with having made clear progress. Conservation organizations, for example, have improved their awareness of the realities faced by indigenous peoples, and these organizations now understand the right of indigenous peoples to chart their own paths. Likewise, indigenous groups have a fuller understanding of the goals of conservation organizations, as well as the strategies such organizations employ for achieving those goals.

An obvious and tangible sign of progress in this area, which has been ably facilitated by groups like Oxfam USA, is the evolution of COICA into an organization now known as the Coalition in Support of Amazonian Peoples and Their Environment. The organizational name change is significant. It means that environmentalists now formally recognize people of the Amazon as key to solving conservation problems in the region. The continued support of U.S. conservation partners also means that the coalition will not disappear. Indeed, the organization now has a secretariat and a full-time coordinator in Washington, D.C.[1]

Despite this progress, some difficult questions remain, particularly relating to sustainable land management. For example, what does sustainable land management mean in practice for indigenous peoples? Does it mean that land must be managed in a "traditional" fashion? If land is not managed in a sustainable fashion—for example, the Huaorani of Ecuador, who promote oil exploration on their newly recognized lands—what is the benefit to conservation? What does "traditional" mean in that kind of situation? Do conservation organizations or national-level indigenous organizations have the right to challenge land use decisions made by local groups of indigenous people?

The Amazon Basin of today is not a museum in which to display indigenous peoples. Neither is it a place hospitable to an unsustainable use of natural resources. Instead, the Amazon is a site of experimentation—where new and innovative approaches to development can, and must, be attempted in the interest of people and conservation. If the alliance between conservationists and the coalition is to prosper, it must continue to produce a vision of development in the Amazon region that is neither romanticized nor unsustainable. With this in mind, the interests of culture and conservation can both be promoted through the continued work of this important alliance.

[1] Private correspondence with Bruce Cabarale, senior associate of the World Resources Institute, July 6, 1995. Bruce has spent several years working with COICA and other indigenous peoples in developing a common framework for conservation and development. His efforts to help in the preparation of this epilogue are much appreciated.

References Cited

COICA. 1988a. "What is COICA?"

COICA. 1988b. To the community of concerned environmentalists.

COICA. 1989a. To the international community: The COICA for the future of the Amazon.

COICA. 1989b. Correspondence between COICA and Ms. Barbara Bramble, National Wildlife Federation, September 30.

COICA. 1990a. Correspondence between COICA and Ms. Barbara Bramble, National Wildlife Federation, January 17.

COICA. 1990b. The Iquitos Declaration. Iquitos, Peru, May 11.

COICA. 1990c. El territorio y la vida indigena como estrategia de defensa de la Amazonia.

Hudson, S. J. 1989. Personal communication with Evaristo Nukguag, COICA president, October 19.

Hudson, S. J. 1990a. Personal communication with Barbara Bramble, National Wildlife Federation, September 21.

Hudson, S. J. 1990b. Personal communication with Wilfrido Aragon, COICA vice president, September 21.

Johnson, M. 1990. Listen to the true caretakers. *Time,* May 21.

Redford, K. 1990. The ecologically noble savage. *Orion* 9(3): 25.

CHAPTER ELEVEN

CONSERVATION AND DEVELOPMENT CONFLICTS IN THE AMAZON BASIN

Michael Painter

Developers and conservationists agree that local participation in project design and management is essential to promoting economic growth through the sustainable use of natural resources. However, reconciling conservation and development goals requires re-evaluation of the ways both groups address their respective areas of concern.

Conservationists, for example, generally view environmental destruction as a problem arising from the relationship between people and their environment rather than as an outcome of relationships among people that affect how the environment is used. As a result, conservation has historically been approached with a combination of educational initiatives, improved technical remedies, and, when these methods fail, state regulation supported by strengthened law enforcement.

In a similar vein, developers have tended to treat local populations as homogeneous. When a good portion of a local population opposes an activity, or when a project goes awry, developers seek solutions through better communication with local people and improved project design and management. They rarely consider the possibility that they already have communicated the benefits of their project perfectly well but that these benefits may conflict with the interests of a significant portion of the local population.

These fundamental problems become clear when examining the gross inequity in access to natural resources that underlies environmental destruction in much of Latin America. To begin with, environmental destruction by small holding farmers is a consequence of their impoverishment relative to other social classes. While development efforts have dealt primarily with natural resource management problems associated with small holders, huge areas have been degraded by wealthy corporate and individual interests. Generally, these large-scale enterprises have received land on concessionary terms from states exercising sovereignty over the area in which they operate, allowing them to treat land as a free good and making it economically advantageous to extract resources unsustainably. Because they institutionalize and exacerbate unequal access to resources, the same policies and practices that give wealthy interests land on concessionary terms are responsible for the impoverishment of small holders. When conservationists and developers fail to address these inequities, their activities may not only fail to promote sustainable development, they may also intensify impoverishment and environmental degradation over the long term.

Agents of Environmental Destruction in Latin America

A major weakness in research and planning with regard to natural resources management in Latin America has been a tendency to extrapolate inappropriately from local situations. This is particularly apparent in the research on environmental degradation by small holders, which forms the bulk of social-science literature on habitat destruction in Latin America. Researchers have given little attention to the destruction associated with large-scale enterprises or to the links between small holder production and the processes of social and economic change caused by large enterprises. This has resulted in analyses that legitimize efforts to blame the rural poor for habitat loss and that justify policies and programs prejudicial to small holders (Wood and Schmink 1979). In the long run, such analyses exacerbate environmental problems by ignoring the devastation associated with large and wealthy enterprises and failing to address problems that promote destructive activities by small holders.

Small Holders

In the Amazon, small holding farmers have been cited both as the major agents of violence against indigenous communities (Whitten 1978; Vickers 1982) and as profligate users of natural resources (Guppy 1984). Yet, the bulk of research on small holders has emphasized that, while they vary considerably in individual knowledge and skill, they are rational users of productive resources and capable of quickly and drastically altering their behavior in order to respond to changing circumstances (Brush 1977; Moran 1974; Barlett 1980). In this context, it is reasonable to ask why these rational resource users destroy the environment on which they depend. Collins (1986) reviewed three cases in the Amazon Basin in which small holder production has been associated with environmental destruction: one along the Brazilian TransAmazon Highway, one in northeastern Ecuador, and the third in southern Peru. In each case, impoverishment arising from the unfavorable position of the small farmer in relation to the regional and national social structure led to destructive patterns of resource use.

In Brazil, Collins found that this impoverishment was caused by a combination of technically inappropriate and poorly administered state incentives that encouraged monocrop rice production to the exclusion of other activities. This led initially to high levels of debt and low rice yields, to which farmers responded by shortening fallow cycles and emphasizing cash crops in an attempt to increase production. The result was increased resource deterioration and debt as well as the establishment of a feedback relationship between debt and declining land productivity. Eventually, farmers unable to pay their debts were bought out by wealthier interests who consolidated the small holdings into larger units, and the former small holder population either went to work as laborers on the larger land holdings or moved deeper into the forest to try again.

In northeastern Ecuador, the cost of purchasing and surveying land put settlers in debt from the time of their arrival. Until they had repaid this debt, farmers could not obtain land titles, which meant that they could not receive credit. This situation forced farmers to maximize short-term profits through rapid conversion of forest to pasture, with no provision for the maintenance of soil fertility. The result was a mutually reinforcing cycle of impoverishment and environmental destruction. Moreover, before many farmers were able to obtain a clear title, they were forced to sell their land to wealthier individuals at a low price and move to new areas of the forest.

In southern Peru, Collins found that because the economy was limited to only a few buyers, farmers had poor access to credit and agricultural inputs. Difficulties in obtaining land titles resulted in a coffee production regimen characterized by low yields and poor quality in which small holding settlers could not earn enough to sever their ties with the farms in the highlands from where they had come. As a result, a pattern of seasonal migration emerged in which family members moved between the highlands and the tropical valleys to carry out agricultural activities in each area. Family labor resources were so insufficient that they were unable to go beyond what was immediately necessary to produce a crop in either area. Consequently, activities to manage soil and water and to maintain the long-term productivity of both areas were neglected. Furthermore, declining productivity in the lowlands created a cycle in which farmers exhausted the land in one area and then moved deeper into the forest to begin anew.

These examples illustrate that small holder impoverishment is a product of resource competition with other interests. In addition, because small holders lack access to development resources enjoyed by other interests, they are unable to accumulate capital. The result is that large farmers, who are better able to mechanize production and who enjoy greater access to development resources from state and international donor agencies, have done much better than small holders, who are constrained by their own family labor resources and diminished capacity to hire additional labor (Painter 1987). Small holders are obliged to respond either by attempting to increase the aggregate production placed on the market or by turning away from agriculture as a means of earning a living. Both of these approaches have led to environmentally destructive production. In eastern Bolivia, for example, small holders are locked in an intense struggle for development resources such as access to markets, agricultural credit, transport enterprises, and lumber operations, and their efforts to secure greater access to resources are greeted with hostility and repressed by violence (Painter 1988). Many settlers in this region have attempted to increase their production by clearing large areas of forest and taking advantage of the flush of productivity that accompanies initial forest removal. Families who practice a production regimen recommended by local farm-aid institutions are able to clear a mean area of approximately 3.5 hectares a year, and comparably sized families who have adopted a more extensive strategy clear from nine to 35 hectares annually (Painter et al. 1984; Painter 1987, 1988).

Increased reliance on off-farm employment also leads to environmentally destructive practices, as it decreases the ability of small holding families to effectively manage soil and water resources. In a review of 10 large-scale studies of rural families throughout Latin America, for example, Deere and Wasserstrom (1980) found that in five of the 10 studies, more than 50 percent of family income was derived from off-farm sources. Seven of the 10 studies showed wages accounting for 30 percent or more of total family income, with the importance of wage labor increasing significantly as landholding size decreased. The growing importance of off-farm income indicates a dilemma confronting rural small holders throughout Latin America. Although they are unable to earn a living through farming, their off-farm earnings are insufficient to let them relinquish their hold on the land. As a result, they must intensify the exploitation of their own labor, devising elaborate strategies for allocating their time and resources among activities that are often spatially distant and temporally competitive. The solution to the labor allocation dilemmas that inevitably arise is to sacrifice long-term resource management for makeshift responses to changing social and economic conditions that vary from one day to the next (Collins 1987, 1988).

Large Enterprises

Throughout Latin America, vast environmental destruction has been associated with the activities of large-scale corporate and individually owned enterprises. In a review of Brazil's Amazon development policy, Hall (1987) points out that between 1975 and 1979, under the Second National Development Plan, 1.7 million hectares of land were sold in 500- to 3,000-hectare plots to both corporations and individuals, more than twice the amount that had been distributed to small holding settlers prior to that time. The most widely studied large-scale enterprises associated with habitat loss in tropical forest areas are cattle ranches (Branford and Glock 1985). Yet mining, industrial logging, and plantation forestry have also been responsible for the degradation of large areas (Goodland 1980, 1985; Hall 1989).

Environmental degradation associated with large, wealthy enterprises often results from state policies that both permit the acquisition of land on concessionary terms and promote productive practices not based on the value of the commodities being produced. Of particular importance are tax policies regarding agricultural income, land, capital gains, and regional or sectional taxes, as well as rules of land allocation and terms for credit. For example, a low tax rate on corporate agricultural profits, combined with generous depreciation provisions, creates incentives to invest in agriculture even though the economic rate of return may be low. Further, land speculation is encouraged by subsidized credit programs—often characterized by negative real interest rates—to which only the wealthy have access (Hecht 1985). Because these policies make land more valuable as an object of speculation than as a resource for commodity production, there is little incentive to conserve it. Instead, the incentive is to occupy as much land as possible, even if it cannot be worked efficiently. In the case of tropical lowlands, there are also incentives to deforest in order to demonstrate possession. During the mid-1960s, for example, the Brazilian government promoted beef cattle production in the Amazon. Their goal was to help make cheap food available for urban workers and to respond to a rapidly expanding international beef market. The government permitted a corporation to invest a substantial portion of its tax liability in Amazonian development projects. Enterprises established before 1966 were exempted from 50 percent of the taxes owed for 12 years, while enterprises established between 1966 and 1972 could receive exemptions of up to 100 percent. Qualifying firms could also import equipment duty free and were exempted from export duties for regional products such as timber. In addition, state governments provided their own inducements, usually in the form of land concessions. Acquiring new land was treated as a development cost that could be substantially written off, making it more profitable to acquire and exploit new land than to develop prior land holdings (Hecht 1985).

In a world of limited development resources, a decision to provide such incentives to the wealthy carries with it a decision not to provide them to the poor. For example, tax incentives and subsidized credit become part of the value of the land and are reflected in land prices. These higher prices either restrict the ability of the poor to acquire legally titled land or encourage them to sell what good land they have. Lacking opportunities to invest the profits, those who sell either move to the cities and become part of the exploding urban population or move onto unclaimed land (land that is frequently unsuitable for annual crop-based agriculture) to begin farming anew (Aramburú 1982). The interests of the poor are thus prejudiced in ways that lead directly to destructive land use and heightened social conflict.

Indirect impacts of the inequitable distribution of wealth—such as the construction of roads, oil pipelines, and hydropower facilities—have also been responsible for widespread environmental destruction in Latin America (Goodland 1980, 1985; International Science and Technology Institute 1980; Rudel 1983). For example, although hydropower plants can generate electricity to support productive activities in distant areas, they have had a dramatic negative environmental impact on the areas where they are constructed. In Brazil's Amazon Basin, hydropower projects have not only caused direct environmental destruction, but they have also drastically affected Native American and Brazilian rural populations by forcing them to relocate. The environmental degradation caused by these population movements has frequently been intensified by national authorities and international donor agencies that refuse to make adequate provision for the relocations.

Similarly, while road construction has allowed immediate, short-term economic growth, it has also been a major contributor to widespread deforestation. Conventional wisdom has held that road construction is an important step toward improving economic opportunities for small holders in tropical forest areas (Nelson 1973). Indeed, Wennergren and Whitaker (1976) have argued that opening roads and encouraging settlement along them is the most cost-effective way for nations to develop their tropical forests. When continued unchecked, however, road building is a major obstacle to achieving sustainable tropical forest development. Fearnside (1985), for example, has argued that the relationship between road building and settler migration is one of the most important forces driving deforestation in Brazil. Building new roads encourages more settlers to enter a region, and the resulting population growth encourages the construction of still more roads. Joly (1982) observed a similar dynamic in Panama, where road construction is frequently justified by improving market access, a concomitant result being the facilitated entrance of new settlers in large numbers. Drawing on research conducted in eastern Ecuador, Rudel (1983) concluded that if establishing sustainable production systems through settlement is a development goal, road construction should follow settlement rather than precede it. While building roads into a new area encourages settlement and rapid economic growth, Rudel found that it also encourages land speculation, poor matching of agricultural activity to soil conditions, and the establishment of unstable, predatory production systems. Stearman (1985) has made similar observations in the Yapacaní settlement area of eastern Bolivia, which grew dramatically when a road and the bridge connecting it to regional urban centers were completed. This economic growth came at the cost of widespread land speculation, and poorer farmers were forced to sell their land and use the money to establish themselves elsewhere, usually in a new area of tropical forest.

The Role of State Policy

State policies that define development in terms of narrow production goals or in support of very specific economic interests have also exacerbated environmental degradation in the Amazon Basin (Goodland 1985; Leonard 1987; Ledec and Goodland 1988). Sustainability of production is frequently not a criterion in planning the allocation of state resources or in formulating policy, and environmental destruction is regarded as the inevitable price of economic growth. In Brazil, for example, a hallmark of Amazonian development policy has been an attempt to use the region for fundamentally contradictory purposes (Bakx 1987; Hall 1987). On the one hand, the government has attempted to promote large-scale agricultural enterprises through the incentives described above, largely to generate export earnings and to take advantage of the expanding international beef market. At the same time, Brazil tried to use its Amazon territory as a "safety valve" to relieve social tensions in areas of land pressure, without addressing underlying land distribution problems. State subsidies for large-scale, export-oriented soybeans, sugar cane, and cattle production in the northeast and south-central regions of the country have continued to push the frontier farther back, displacing many small farmers and compelling them to seek new lands in the Amazon. Through aggressive road construction, the state has encouraged this migration as a means of populating and asserting national sovereignty over the Amazon as well as avoiding the need to address gross inequities in resource distribution in the migrants' home areas. Yet while government has encouraged settlement, it has declined to provide either a way for settlers to secure title to their new landholdings or incentives for them to maintain and improve the productive potential of that land. Instead, state-encouraged investments focus on cattle ranching, the extraction of tropical forest products, and coffee, cocoa, and rubber production—all to supply export markets. The result has been vast inequities in resource distribution similar to those in other parts of the country that drove migration into the Amazon.

In Peru, the government has promoted settlement of the "high jungle" on the eastern Andean slopes to relieve social and economic pressures in the nation's highland agricultural regions (Aramburú 1982). The first and second Belaúnde administrations (1963–68, 1980–85) in particular focused on expanding tropical forest production as a means of promoting economic growth in lieu of addressing resource distribution issues elsewhere in the country. The state's haste to make the tropical forest more accessible to settlers, cattle ranchers, timber companies, and other interests led to the construction of a very expensive and poorly planned infrastructure, which is not likely to survive long on the region's steep slopes without continued substantial investment. Large areas of land were earmarked for agriculture without regard to whether or not they were appropriate. Moreover, the state gave only begrudging recognition to the fact that much of the land to be incorporated into tropical forest development projects was already occupied by Native Americans (Stocks 1987).

Central America differs from South America in that expanding tropical forest production has not been explicitly linked to the achievement of national development goals (Collins and Painter 1986). Yet Central American nations have promoted deforestation throughout the region in response to a growing export market for beef in the United States and Europe. These states have encouraged cattle production by concentrating bank credits, technical assistance, and infrastructure development to support this industry to the detriment of other types of agricultural activities. This policy has been consistent with sound tropical forest management (Myers 1981; JRB Associates 1982; DeWalt 1983; Nations and Komer 1983).

Conclusion: The Challenge of Local Participation

Several challenges face those attempting to promote local participation in sustainable resource use and economic growth in Latin America. First, conservationists and developers alike must sharpen their abilities to place national resource competition in a historical context in order to identify and describe the social and economic underpinnings of resource degradation. Second, designs for co-managing conservation and development must be based on an explicit understanding of the values promoted through particular types of production regimens and institutional arrangements. There are no universal solutions. As can be seen from the examples cited, there is nothing inherent in either small holder production or large-scale development that makes one or the other destructive. Instead, environmental destruction and economic impoverishment are consequences of relationships among people with diverse and conflicting economic interests. In areas like the Amazon Basin, where small holding settlers exist side-by-side with large lumber companies and multinational manufacturers, "local participation" quickly becomes a hollow concept unless participation is distinctly defined and the institutional arrangements made clear. Only then does the issue of resource access, which underlies development and environmental destruction, emerge. And only then can we speak meaningfully of local participation, where that participation involves collective decision making about the kind of world we wish to build through exploiting and/or conserving natural resources.

Acknowledgments

This paper was prepared with support from the Cooperative Agreement on Settlement and Resource Systems Analysis of the Institute for Development Anthropology, Clark University, and the U.S. Agency for International Development. Vivan Carlip, Katy Moran, and participants in the National Zoological Park's symposium "Culture: The Missing Element in Conservation and Development" provided helpful comments on previous versions of the paper. The views expressed are those of the author, however, and do not necessarily reflect positions of any of the above-named people or institutions.

References Cited

Aramburú, C. E. 1982. Expansión de la frontera agraria y demográfica en la selva alta peruana. In *Colonización en la Amazonía*, C. E. Aramburú, E. Bedoya, and J. Recharte, eds. 1–39. Lima, Peru: Centro de Investigación y Promoción Amazónica.

Bakx, K. 1987. Planning agrarian reform: Amazonian settlement projects, 1970–86. *Development and Change* 18: 533–555.

Barlett, P. 1980. Adaptive strategies in peasant agricultural production. *Annual Review of Anthropology* 9: 545–573.

Branford, S., and O. Glock. 1985. *The last frontier: Fighting over land in the Amazon*. London: Zed Books.

Brush, S. B. 1977. *Mountain, field, and family: The economy and human ecology of an Andean valley*. Philadelphia: University of Pennsylvania Press.

Collins, J. L. 1986. Smallholder settlement of tropical South America: The social causes of ecological destruction. *Human Organization* 45: 1–10.

Collins, J. L. 1987. Labor scarcity and ecological change. In *Lands at risk in the Third World: Local-level perspectives*, P. D. Little and M. M. Horowitz, eds. 19–37. Boulder, Colo.: Westview Press.

Collins, J. L. 1988. *Unseasonal migrations: The effects of rural labor scarcity in Peru*. Princeton, N.J.: Princeton University Press.

Collins, J. L. and M. Painter. 1986. *Settlement and deforestation in Central America: A discussion of development issues*. Binghamton, N.Y.: Institute for Development Anthropology.

Deere, C. D., and R. Wasserstrom. 1980. *Ingreso familiar y trabajo no agrícola entre los pequeños productores internacional sobre la producción agropecuaria y forestal en zonas de ladera en América Latina*. Turrialba, Costa Rica.

DeWalt, B. 1983. The cattle are eating the forest. *Bulletin of the Atomic Scientists* 39: 18–23.

Fearnside, P. M. 1985. Environmental change and deforestation in the Brazilian Amazon. In *Change in the Amazon Basin, Vol. 1: Man's impact on forests and rivers*, J. Hemming, ed. 70–89. Manchester, United Kingdom: University of Manchester Press.

Goodland, R. J. A. 1980. Environmental ranking of Amazonian development projects in Brazil. *Environmental Conservation* 7: 9–26.

Goodland, R. J. A. 1985. Brazil's environmental progress in Amazonian development. In *Change in the Amazon Basin, Vol. 1: Man's impact on forests and rivers*, J. Hemming, ed. 3–35. Manchester, United Kingdom: University of Manchester Press.

Guppy, N. 1984. Tropical deforestation: A global view. *Foreign Affairs* 62: 928–965.

Hall, A. 1987. Agrarian crisis in Brazilian Amazonia: The Grande Carajás Programme. *Journal of Development Studies* 23: 522–552.

Hall, A. L. 1989. *Developing Amazonia: Deforestation and social conflict in Brazil's Carajás Programme*. Manchester, United Kingdom: Manchester University Press.

Hecht, S. B. 1985. Environment, development and politics: Capital accumulation and the livestock sector in Eastern Amazonia. *World Development* 13: 663–684.

International Science and Technology Institute. 1980. *Panamá: Condiciones del medio ambiente y de los recursos naturales*. Washington, D.C.: International Science and Technology Institute.

Joly, L. G. 1982. La migración de los interioranos hacia la Costa Abajo. In *Colonización y destrucción de bosques en Panamá*, S. Heckadon Moreno and A. McKay, eds. 63–80. Panamá: Asociación Panameña de Antropología.

JRB Associates. 1982. *Honduras: Country environmental profile*. McLean, Va.: JRB Associates.

Ledec, M., and R. J. A. Goodland. 1988. Epilogue: An environmental perspective on tropical land settlement. In *The human ecology of tropical land settlement in Latin America*, D. Schumann and W. Partridge, eds. Boulder, Colo.: Westview Press.

Leonard, H. J. 1987. *Natural resources and economic development in Central America: A regional environmental profile.* New Brunswick, N.J.: Transaction Books.

Moran, E. 1974. The adaptive strategy of the Amazonian Caboclo. In *Man in the Amazon*, C. Wagley, ed. 136–159. Gainesville: University of Florida Press.

Myers, N. 1981. The hamburger connection: How Central America's forests become North America's hamburgers. *Ambio* 10: 3–8.

Nations, J. D., and D. I. Komer. 1983. Rainforests and the hamburger society. *Environment* 25: 12–25.

Nelson, M. 1973. *The development of tropical lands: Policy issues in Latin America.* Baltimore, Md.: Johns Hopkins University Press.

Painter, M. 1987. Unequal exchange: The dynamics of settler impoverishment and environmental destruction in lowland Bolivia. In *Lands at risk in the Third World: Local-level perspectives*, P. D. Little and M. M. Horowitz, eds. 164–191. Boulder, Colo.: Westview Press.

Painter, M. 1988. Competition and conflict in the Bolivian lowlands: Ethnicity and social class formation. Paper presented at the annual meeting of the American Anthropological Association, Phoenix, Ariz., November.

Painter, M., C. A. Perez-Crespo, M. Llanos Albornóz, S. Hamilton, and W. Partridge. 1984. New lands settlement and regional development: The case of San Julian, Bolivia. Working Paper 15. Binghamton, N.Y.: Institute for Development Anthropology.

Perez-Crespo, C. A. 1991. Migration and the breakdown of a peasant economy in central Bolivia. Working Paper 82. Binghamton, N.Y.: Institute for Development Anthropology.

Rudel, T. K. 1983. Roads, speculators and colonization in the Ecuadorian Amazon. *Human Ecology* 11: 385–403.

Stearman, A. M. 1985. Colonization in Santa Cruz, Bolivia: A comparative study of the Yapacaní and San Julián projects. In *Frontier expansion in Amazonia*, M. Schmink and C. Woods, eds. 231–260. Gainesville: University of Florida Press.

Stocks, A. 1987. Tropical forest development in Peru. *Development Anthropology Network* 5: 1–8.

Vickers, W. T. 1982. Development and Amazonian Indians: The Aguarico case and some general principles. In *The dilemma of Amazonian development*, E. Moran, ed. 25–50. Boulder, Colo.: Westview Press.

Wennergren, E. B., and M. Whitaker. 1976. Investment in access roads and spontaneous colonization: Additional evidence from Bolivia. *Land Economics* 52: 88–95.

Whitten, N. 1978. Amazonian Ecuador: An ethnic interface in ecological, social, and ideological perspectives. Document No. 34. Copenhagen: International Work Group for Indigenous Affirs.

Wood, C., and M. Schmink. 1979. Blaming the victim: Small farmer production in the Amazon colonization project. *Studies in Third World Societies* 7: 77–93.

CHAPTER TWELVE

DEBT-FOR-NATURE SWAPS: U.S. POLICY ISSUES AND OPTIONS

Katy Moran

The idea that indebted developing countries be allowed to exchange their debt for the protection of natural resources, particularly tropical forests, was first proposed by Thomas Lovejoy in 1984 (Lovejoy 1984). Since then, more than $100 million worth of debt-for-nature swaps have taken place, and this visionary concept has become a powerful tool for conservation. As the United States considers expanding this initiative, however, policy makers must examine thoroughly its benefits and constraints and clearly define the options available for implementation.

Nature of the Debt

During the inflationary economic environment of the 1970s, lesser developed countries (LDCs) borrowed heavily from three types of creditors that were eager to encourage economic development: commercial banks, multilateral development banks (MDBs), and bilateral foreign-assistance programs. However, oil price shocks in 1973 and 1979 and a U.S. recession in 1981 drastically altered the economic conditions affecting payment of these debts. With rising interest rates, an appreciating dollar, and declining commodity prices, developing countries soon found it difficult to pay interest on the debts (U.S. Congress 1986). In August 1982, the Mexican government revealed that it could not service its $80 billion debt; by the end of 1983, 42 other countries were also behind on their payments.

In response, many of these nations resorted to borrowing from the International Monetary Fund (IMF), which grants short-term loans to financially troubled countries if they agree to specific economic-reform programs (Hino 1988). As a result, fiscal austerity and export programs were ordered by the IMF to reform economic conditions in countries that applied for funds to service their external debt. Austerity programs in turn made imports more expensive to debtor countries by devaluating local currency and eliminating subsidies. These currency devaluations increased import prices and stimulated inflation. After three devaluations over a 13-month period, Philippine families, for instance, paid 80 percent more for the same basket of groceries in 1984 than they had in 1983. Reduced government subsidies created a shortage in fertilizers and other agricultural inputs for small farmers, causing food shortages and malnutrition among the rural poor. And when governments froze wages and reduced expenditures by eliminating social-welfare programs, education and health services also declined (Debt Crisis Network 1985).

Since loan payments must be paid in U.S. dollars or another hard currency, the IMF also required debtor countries to increase their production of export commodities and to develop nontraditional exports to trade for hard currency (Bird 1987). As a result, developing countries flooded export markets with products such as coffee, cocoa, clothing, coconuts, and copper, driving down prices and causing world trade in these products to stagnate between 1980 and 1984. For example, while world sugar prices remained at 5 to 6 cents a pound in early 1985, production costs in the Philippines rose to 12 to 14 cents a pound.

In order to promote exports, ecologically unstable monocultures began to replace diverse and stable subsistence agriculture throughout the developing world. The resulting loss of staple food crops led to increased malnutrition. In short, IMF austerity and export programs only served to create greater hardships for LDCs and did nothing to improve their economies. According to the World Development Report of 1988, resource transfers from industrial countries shifted from a capital inflow of $147 billion between 1977 and 1982 to a capital outflow of $85 billion between 1982 and 1988 (World Bank 1988). Today, more money is going out of developing countries for debt payments than is going into them for development.

The Impact of LDC Debt on the U.S. Economy

Debt creates crises in many sectors, including trade, industry, banking, and farming, for both creditor and borrower countries. Since about a third of U.S. trade is with the developing world, IMF import restrictions in the 1970s led to massive job losses in U.S. export-oriented industries. In 1985, Wharton Economic Forecasting Associates testified before the Joint Economics Committee of the U.S. Congress that in one year the United States lost 800,000 jobs as a result of the Latin American debt crisis alone. U.S. farmers were particularly affected, as increased LDC exports directly competed with their corn, rice, and soybeans. Such crops flooded world markets, driving prices down and undermining the position of farmers everywhere. And farmers in both the United States and developing countries suffered from the high and fluctuating interest rates generated by U.S. budget deficits and an unstable international economic system (Debt Crisis Network 1985).

Who Owes What to Whom?

Seven countries account for almost half the $1.3 trillion LDC debt: Mexico, Brazil, Argentina, and Venezuela in Latin America, and South Korea, Indonesia, and the Philippines in Asia. Each owes more than $25 billion, mostly to commercial banks that hold short-term loans with high interest rates. The default of one of these "Big Seven" debtors would shake the international financial system; their collective default could destroy it. Middle-range debtors include two dozen African nations plus Costa Rica, El Salvador, Guatemala, Honduras, and Nicaragua in Central America, and Bolivia, Peru, Ecuador, and Chile in South America. While these countries owe large sums in proportion to their capacity to repay, their default would not trigger a worldwide financial crisis. The third group of debtors consists of the very poorest African countries. They owe official creditors, both multilateral and bilateral, that grant low-interest-rate loans with long-term payment schedules. Although they do not have large debts because commercial banks regard them as poor credit risks, they are still seriously affected by the international financial system (Wertman 1986). Today, most of the capital of developing nations goes to pay the almost $1.3 trillion external debt owed to developed nations. Not only is there no money left for economic growth, but economic policies such as the required IMF export emphasis are also depleting the natural resource base upon which the growth of the developing world ultimately depends.

Social and Environmental Impacts of Debt and Deforestation

All natural resources are affected by developing countries' debt. However, tropical forests and the people who depend on them for their subsistence are suffering the most. Massive tropical deforestation has created many difficult-to-solve socioeconomic problems, which are intensifying relentlessly each day. Poverty, overpopulation, inequitable land distribution, poor land use and land tenure policy, and inappropriate development all lead to a vicious cycle of poverty and pressure on natural resources. National and international policies to generate hard currency for debt payments promote mining, logging, cash-crop monocultures, and expanded cattle production—the leading causes of tropical forest deforestation (Petesch 1990). These links between debt and deforestation demonstrate that it is impossible to isolate economic, social, and environmental problems and that solutions require a recognition of those interrelationships (Downing and Kushner 1988). In the past, we feared the impact of economic growth on the environment, but today we must also recognize that environmental stress—particularly deforestation—threatens future economic prospects worldwide.

Commercial Bank Debt

The "first generation" of debt-for-nature swaps involved commercial bank debt (Conservation International 1989). Because many commercial banks collect neither interest nor principal payments for LDC debt, they have developed a secondary market in which banks trade or sell foreign debt at a discounted rate to minimize their losses. Commercial debt has thus been sold or donated to environmental nongovernmental organizations (NGOs) through this market.

The first debt-for-nature swap took place in July 1987 between Conservation International (CI), a U.S.-based NGO, and the government of Bolivia. CI was able to purchase $650,000 worth of deeply discounted Bolivian debt for $100,000 on the secondary market and then cancel the debt in return for a plan to manage almost four million acres of tropical forest in the Bolivian Amazon. CI is the first to acknowledge that its pioneer debt-for-nature swap was not without problems, but it did effectively pave the way for other conservation NGOs that soon followed its lead. In developing countries, local NGOs such as Fundación de Parques Nationales in Costa Rica, Fundación Natura in Ecuador, and the Haribon Foundation in the Philippines have facilitated nearly $100 million of U.S. debt retirement through debt-for-nature swaps. Their U.S.-based counterparts, such as CI, World Wildlife Fund, and The Nature Conservancy, have also facilitated the financing of a wide range of activities, including the training of local scientists and land managers and management of buffer zones surrounding protected areas (Cody 1990).

The impetus for a swap generally originates with a local NGO that enlists the help of a U.S.-based NGO to raise funds to purchase a portion of its country's commercial bank debt. The U.S. organization then negotiates with a U.S. commercial bank to either sell at a deep discount (through the secondary market) or donate the debt to the NGO. The U.S. NGO also negotiates with the borrower country on the terms of settlement and on the environmental activity suggested by the local NGO. The borrower country typically agrees to pay some or all of the value of the loan to the U.S. NGO in the form of long-term interest-bearing bonds.

To date, debt swaps have been narrow in scope, creating a misconception of their purpose and potential. Some observers have charged "ecological imperialism," with swaps criticized as an exchange of debt for ownership of sovereign territory. In fact, in the first generation of swaps, land ownership never changed. Likewise, the impetus for the swaps emerged from the debtor countries, and funds have been managed by local organizations structured to meet local conservation priorities (Bramble and Millikan 1990).

Multilateral Development Bank Debt

In 1987 Congressman John Porter (R-Ill.) took the first U.S. legislative action to alleviate debt and deforestation problems. Porter's Tropical Forest Protection Act (H.R. 3010 and H.R. 1704 during the 100th and 101st Congresses, respectively) called on the U.S. executive director of the World Bank and other multilateral development banks to allow a country with MDB loans to convert part of its debt payments into local currency for conservation projects. The bill also contained provisions to strengthen NGOs involved in grass-roots environmental protection and resource management in developing countries (Moran 1992). The World Bank responded to Porter's bill by stating that any form of debt rescheduling or restructuring would undermine its credit rating and that rescheduling is forbidden by its charter. However, many felt that debt-for-nature swaps offered the bank an opportunity to demonstrate concrete commitment to improving and mitigating admitted negative environmental consequences of its past funding decisions. In 1988, bank president Barber Conable echoed these sentiments by publicly stating the bank's commitment to improve the environmental quality of its loans. "If the bank has been part of the [environmental] problem in the past, I intend to make it a leader in finding solutions," Conable stated (Holden 1988). During the 101st Congress, Representative Porter's bill was incorporated into H.R. 2494. The bill passed and was signed into law (PL 101-240) by President Bush on December 19, 1989, as the International Development and Finance Act of 1989. International NGOs and executive directors of MDBs are now promoting efforts to use multilateral bank debt for swaps.

Bilateral Debt

At a February 1990, summit between U.S. president George Bush and the presidents of Colombia, Peru, and Bolivia, the potential scale of debt swaps increased dramatically. Announced by the president on June 27, 1990, the meeting's outcome was the Enterprise for the Americas Initiative (EAI). The goal of this initiative was to forge an "economic partnership" within the Western Hemisphere through a plan involving trades, investment, and debt. Under the EAI, if a Latin American or Caribbean country took steps toward economic, trade, and investment reforms, the United States would reduce the country's official bilateral debt. By the early 1990s, the countries affected by EAI owed a total of nearly $12 billion to the United States in concessionary debt—including Food for Peace and U.S. Agency for International Development loans—as well as market-rate debt that includes Export-Import Bank and Commodity Credit Corporation loans.

To be eligible for debt reduction, a debtor country must have plans to satisfy four conditions: economic reforms through the World Bank, economic reforms through the International Monetary Fund (IMF), investment reforms through the Inter-American Development Bank, and debt reduction programs with commercial bank lenders. If a country has complied with these conditions, its principal can be reduced by an average of 50 percent and, in some countries, by as much as 85 percent. The reduction is determined on a case-by-case basis, and the remaining principal must be paid in dollars over a period of 20 to 30 years. The debtor country thus receives a reduction in what it owes, but not in the amount it currently pays. To avoid any impact on the U.S. budget, the debtor must also continue to make historical principal payments. In this way, the process remains neutral to the U.S. budget and requires no new appropriation. The debtor then pays a concessionary interest rate of 2.5 percent on its reduced debt in local currency, which is placed in a local environmental fund, and local-currency interest payments gradually decrease as principal diminishes. Debtor countries have financial incentives to participate in the EAI. Their principals are substantially reduced, interest payments can be paid in local currency rather than dollars, and they do not continue to accumulate principal and interest that lead to an ever-mounting debt burden.

Despite these benefits, many Latin American and U.S. environmental NGOs criticize the EAI. While they recognize that the initiative increases financing for debt-for-nature swaps, they are concerned that its conditions for economic reform make environmental concerns secondary. For example, a World Bank evaluation of the impact of its economic reform programs failed to include environmental effects. More important, policies of the IMF, unlike those initiated by Conable at the World Bank, lacked an institutional mandate to assess the environmental and social impact of its actions. Thus, many question whether the conditions for economic reform are consistent with the environmental objectives of the EAI and the process of sustainable development. Despite these concerns, intense lobbying by environmental NGOs eased some of the stringent conditions of the original administration bill and resulted in passage of part of the EAI initiative. The Farm Bill (S. 2830, S. Report 101-357, H. Report 101-569, Conf. Report 101-916), that was signed into law by President Bush in November 1990 authorized $1.7 billion of U.S. debt in Latin America as eligible for debt reduction.

Future Prospects

The "second generation" of debt-for-nature swaps has enlarged the scale of swaps and more clearly defined the incentives and constraints surrounding them. In 1989, for example, U.S. NGOs lobbied for a provision in the EAI mandating that local NGOs in debtor countries play a key role in implementing and managing funded programs. Strengthening NGO institutions in developing countries may yield potent results in Latin American nations with fragile new democracies, and such action is crucially needed to focus funds, political power, and personnel to those who can best understand and manage local resource needs. In addition, as bilateral debt has also begun to play a major role in financing debt-for-nature swaps, the World Bank has been recognized as the institution to further increase the scale of future swaps through debt restructuring in developing countries.

Despite these incentives to increase the scale of swaps, there are still many people who argue that swaps "legitimize" debt that was negotiated by dictators for their own benefit and that LDCs today struggle to rule democratically under the burden of unjust debt. They feel that, given the severe debt problems, debt forgiveness is the real issue at hand and that swaps only distract from it. Proponents, however, argue that swaps were never intended to solve the debt crisis, but were designed to free funds for much needed conservation programs. Because second-generation swaps will dramatically expand the scale of debt reduction, another problem may be that bank debt will have a higher value for "free riders." In other words, banks that have not participated in debt reduction may still benefit from debt-for-nature swaps because the debt will become more valuable as it becomes more likely to be paid. If this happens, it will be reflected in the secondary market for commercial bank debt, and NGOs may lose the advantage of the large discount that gives them leverage for their contributions.

Conclusion

There are still many unanswered questions surrounding the Enterprise for the Americas Initiative. Are eligibility criteria too rigid, and could the United States itself meet them? Could these criteria disqualify or discourage countries that merit help? Does the discretion vested in the U.S. president to waive eligibility requirements yield too much congressional control of the EAI process? How can eligibility conditions be harmonized with environmental protection? Does the EAI set unwanted precedents to forgive other debt? Have U.S. budget effects been fully accounted for? Should the use of environmental funds be broadened to include development? Exactly what kind of environmental activities have first-generation swaps accomplished, and what has been their impact on local people?

Despite questions, two things are quite clear. Debt-for-nature swaps offer critical time that is needed to secure protection for tropical ecosystems, and they also promote the sustainable use of natural resources necessary for the economic development of LDCs. It is unrealistic to expect developing countries to halt deforestation for environmental reasons alone. The immediate priority of developing countries today is the debt crisis, and existence of the secondary market proves that many debts are not being serviced and will never be paid in full (Eberstadt 1988). Debt-for-nature swaps provide a critically needed first step in addressing the relationship between these debt issues and the mounting problems of deforestation and environmental degradation.

Epilogue

Since this chapter was written, U.S. conservation organizations have continued to rely heavily on debt-for-nature swaps. These have occurred worldwide but have focused mainly on the Latin American tropics. Many other industrialized countries have followed the U.S. lead, using their discounted debt to finance environmental projects in developing countries. In 1994, for example, a $500,000 Canadian bilateral debt donation provided funds for Peruvian parks.

In contrast to earlier days of debt swaps, the potential for using commercial bank debt today is less because stronger debt markets have made that debt more valuable and less likely to be discounted. Since passage of the EAI, bilateral debt has become the most important source of funds for debt-for-nature swaps. As of January 1993, the United States had reduced its bilateral debt to seven Latin American countries by $875 million and created local-currency funds for the environment and children's health of $154 million. In 1994, numerous bilateral swaps were under negotiation for national environmental funds in various Latin American and Caribbean countries.

The Debt-for-Development Coalition (DDC), a nonprofit organization that was established in 1991 with funds from the U.S. Agency for International Development, has completed about 100 transactions for developmental, environmental, and social welfare organizations based in both developed and developing countries. These transactions have reduced external debt by almost $70 million and have generated more than $14.5 million in additional developmental resources. In addition, the World Bank now funds commercial external debt reduction programs. For example, under a Bank-financed debt buy-back in July 1994, Zambia reduced its debt by almost $85 million. In return for the debt cancellation, over $5 million in local currency will be shared by 13 Zambian NGOs for a variety of health, environmental, education, low-income housing, and micro-enterprise development projects.

Many questions remain, however, regarding these successes and the lessons learned since the first debt-for-nature swap. There is still no clear model for a swap mechanism. Instead, a wide variety of innovative financial mechanisms tailored to the needs of debtor countries and debt holders continues to evolve.

New partnerships between local and national NGOs in debtor countries have increased the value, awareness, and number of the NGOs in developing counties and made debt swaps more responsive to local needs. In addition, local currency funds have created endowments for unprecedented cash flows for NGOs for several years into the future, enabling long-term planning for both projects and job security. This has resulted in strengthened infrastructure for both NGOs and governments, thus empowering debtor countries and NGOs to negotiate their own swaps in the future. There is concern, however, that these sophisticated financial processes may in fact act to cut out the grassroots NGOs who do the actual work implementing the swaps. The top-down structure of debt-for-nature swaps, which responds to the debt problems of governments and financial institutions without necessarily considering the needs of local people, leaves many questions on their true impact at the local level. It is still too early to judge whether the stated purpose of each swap has been achieved. The first serious study to evaluate the local impact of debt swaps was scheduled for publication in 1995.

References Cited

Bird, G. R. 1987. *International financial policy and economic development: A disaggregated approach.* New York: St. Martin Press.

Bramble, B. J., and B. H. Millikan. 1990. *External debt, democratization, and natural resources in developing countries: The case of Brazil.* Washington, D.C.: National Wildlife Federation.

Cody, B. 1990. Debt-for-nature swaps in developing countries: An overview of recent conservation efforts. Congressional Research Service Report for Congress. 88–647 EN. Washington, D.C.: Library of Congress.

Conservation International. 1989. *The debt-for-nature exchange: A toll for international conservation.* Washington, D.C.: Conservation International.

Debt Crisis Network. 1985. *From debt to development.* Washington, D.C.: Institute for Policy Studies.

Downing, T. E., and G. Kushner. 1988. *Human rights and anthropology.* Cambridge, Mass.: Cultural Survival, Inc.

Eberstadt, N. N. 1988. How creditworthy is the World Bank? *New York Times*, March 1.

Hino, H. 1988. IMF-World Bank collaboration. *Finance and Development* 23: 10–14.

Holden, C. 1988. The greening of the World Bank. *Science* 240: 610.

Lovejoy, T. E. 1988. Nothing, nothing at all? Paper presented at the annual meeting of the American Institute of Biological Sciences, University of California at Davis, August 1988.

Lovejoy, T. E. 1984. Aid debtor nations' ecology. *New York Times*, October 4.

Moran, K. 1992. Debt-for-nature swaps: A response to debt and deforestation in developing countries? In *Development or destruction? The conversion of forests to pastures in Latin America,* Theodore E. Downing et al., eds. Boulder, Colo.: Westview Press.

Petesch, P. 1990. Tropical forests: Conservation with development? Overseas Development Council Policy Paper No. 4. Washington, D.C.: Overseas Development Council.

U.S. Congress. 1986. Managing the debt problem. January 23 Hearing, Joint Economics Committee, Subcommittee on Economic Goals and Intergovernmental Policy, 99th Congress, 2nd Session. Washington, D.C.: GPO.

Wertman, P. 1986. *The international debt problem: Options for solution.* Washington, D.C.: Congressional Research Service, Library of Congress.

World Bank. 1988. *1988 world development report.* New York: Oxford Press.

CONTRIBUTORS

Lou Ann Dietz, World Wildlife Fund, Washington, D.C.

Harvey A. Feit, Department of Anthropology, McMaster University, Hamilton, Ontario, Canada

Jere L. Gilles, Department of Rural Sociology, University of Missouri, Columbia, Missouri

Robert J. Hoage, National Zoological Park, Smithsonian Institution, Washington, D.C.

Benita J. Howell, Department of Anthropology, University of Tennessee, Knoxville, Tennessee

Stewart J. Hudson, National Wildlife Federation, Washington, D.C.

Diane O'Reilly Lill, Department of Zoology, University of Maryland, College Park, Maryland

Bonnie J. McCay, Department of Human Ecology, Rutgers University, New Brunswick, New Jersey

Jeffrey A. McNeely, Deputy Director General for Conservation, IUCN, Gland, Switzerland

Katy Moran, Healing Forest Conservancy, Washington, D.C.

Michael Painter, Institute for Development Anthropology, Binghamton, New York

Darrell A. Posey, Oxford, United Kingdom

Michael H. Robinson, National Zoological Park, Smithsonian Institution, Washington, D.C.

Rasanayagam Rudran, Conservation and Research Center, National Zoological Park, Smithsonian Institution, Washington, D.C.

R. Michael Wright, African Wildlife Foundation, Washington, D.C.